A YARN OF WAR

BRIGADIER-GENERAL A. H. LEGGETT, C.M.G., D.S.O.

A
YARN OF WAR

PALESTINE AND FRANCE
1917–1918

BY
E. R. B.

The Naval & Military Press Ltd

Published by

The Naval & Military Press Ltd
Unit 5 Riverside, Brambleside
Bellbrook Industrial Estate
Uckfield, East Sussex
TN22 1QQ England

Tel: +44 (0)1825 749494

www.naval-military-press.com
www.nmarchive.com

In reprinting in facsimile from the original, any imperfections are inevitably reproduced and the quality may fall short of modern type and cartographic standards.

TO

THE BEST OF

ALL GOOD COMRADES

ORDER

BY

AN ERSTWHILE OFFICER

Reference Maps,
  see pages 56, 116, 144,   September, 1919.
     216, 232.

1. The Situation is such that, owing to the innumerable calls on its resources, Memory will be unable to retain possession of more than a few stray threads of War unless immediate assistance is forthcoming.

2. The Intention is therefore to catch together a number of loose strands tacked on to incidents important and trivial, and spin, as a reinforcement to Memory, the yarn which is woven into these pages.

3. Readers will move to the area of operations (preferably a deep armchair in which it may be possible to fall asleep) and attack the pages in short rushes. A preliminary preparation of liquid fire from behind a smoke screen will be found beneficial to morale.

4. In view of probable casualties arrangements should be made for a supply of Medical Comforts.

5. Headquarters will be established in the rear of the Operation Area, whither acknowledgment and reports should be forwarded.

  Issued by Post
  to a few of
  those concerned.   E. R. B.

Lured by the Great Adventure, playing the Greatest Game ;
   Out where the sands are burning red ;
Plodding through the Desert, sleeping 'neath the stars ;
   Guarded by the Outposts on ahead.

Crawling about in the darkness out beyond the wire,
   Bombs and Bayonets handy for the fight ;
Listening for the rustle of the grass which says " Beware,
   An enemy patrol is out to-night."

Bivouacked deep in a wadi, shared with a million flies,
   Here where the Army calls " In Rest " ;
Digging trenches half the night, working all the day—
   Seems a sort of far-fetched kind of jest.

Rushing an enemy strongpoint, led by a fierce barrage,
   Hell let loose from rifle, bomb and gun ;
Carrying in relays loads of shovels, picks and wire
   Needed to consolidate what's won.

Right in the van of the Army, chasing a wily foe,
   Railhead lagging many miles behind ;
Rations short and Water scarce, Khamseen blowing hot,
   March and fight—the constant daily grind.

Passing the ancient landmarks, dreaming of times gone by,
   Living 'mid the hardships of To-day ;
Numbers sadly thinning, for a silent rearguard rests
   Where the wooden crosses mark the way.

West to the wild storm centre, amid the miasma of War,
  There in time to share the final din ;
Bringing help, and laying lusty shoulders to the wheel
  For the crowning push that's bound to win.

Carters and Plumbers and Miners, Clerks from the office stool,
  Every type that mem'ry can recall,
Throw the dice and back their luck, cheerful to the last,
  Playing out the Greatest Game of all.

CONTENTS

THE ROAD TO THE FRONT.

PAGE

Overland to Marseilles—A Complete Guide to the duties of Ship's Adjutant—Life on a " Trooper "—Perquisites at Malta—Alexandria—The Campaign against Grease—To the Promised Land *via* Kantara and Romani—Of the Comforts and Convenience of Military Travel,   1

IN FRONT OF GAZA.

The Second Battle of Gaza : April, 1917—Consolidation—How to Build a Tank—Slag Heap—A new Recipe for Scones—The use of the Bayonet in War—Leave—The Pleasures of Patrolling—The Cost of Popularity—The Complete Method of Rationing an Infantry Brigade—Intensive Training—Sheikh Ajlin—Some Preparations for Battle—A Scandal—The Third Battle of Gaza : November, 1917—Chits -   18

THROUGH THE LAND OF THE PHILISTINES.

A Strategical Digression—Wadi Hesi—A Reconnaissance by Mounted Infantry—To Askalon and Mejdel—In the Market-place of Ashdod—Burkah—" Hide and Seek " with the Battalion—A Musical Comedy at Ekron—A Full Account of the History and Glories of Ramleh   62

CONTENTS

AMONG THE HILLS.

PAGE

The Joys of Night Marching—Some Peculiarities of Roman Roads—Beit Likia—The Spirit of the Men—Wanderings among the Hilltops—To Kubeibeh (Emmaus) and Neby Samwil—Eventful Days—Bully Beef and Biscuits—A Calm between Two Storms—Beit Sira—Back to the Plains - - - - - 89

IN THE LAND OF THE ORANGE GROVES.

Adventures with a Wadi and Some Camels—Sarona and its Orange Groves—The Forcing of the Auja—On the Plain of Sharon—Expectations and Realities of Christmas Eve in the Holy Land—How to Conduct an Alarm with full Scenic Effect - - - - 118

JERUSALEM AND BETHLEHEM.

The Ride from Sarona—Some Slight Idea of the Hills—A Haggis in the Holy City—A Tour of the Holy Places—From the Via Dolorosa to the Church of the Sepulchre—Bethlehem and the Church of the Holy Nativity - - - - - - - - - 150

HERE AND THERE.

Back to Balutah—The Return of Spring—An Airman's Souvenirs—The Brigade Mascot—Up the Nile—A Week-end with the Ptolemies—The Great Barrage - 162

WESTWARD HO!

Rumours—Farewell to Palestine—H.M.T. "Canberra"—Final Reconnaissances at Alexandria—The Division at Sea - - - - - - - - - 175

CONTENTS

FRANCE.

From Marseilles to the Backmost Area—Lessons in Frightfulness—At Vimy Ridge—Au Revoir to the 52nd Division—P.P.C. Letters—Home Leave—To Flanders and the 34th Division—To another Front by train, bus, and march route—With the French and Americans—Through the Forests—On the Fringe of Battle—In the Care of the French Medical Services—Exploits with a Foreign Tongue—A British Red-Cross Hospital in France—Home - - - - 187

SIDE SHOWS.

A Field General Court Martial - - - - - 244

A Company Concert in Palestine - - - - - 246

ILLUSTRATIONS

	PAGE
Brigadier-General A. H. Leggett, C.M.G., D.S.O. Frontispiece.	
Base Depot at Mustapha, near Alexandria	4
Races at the Sporting Club, Alexandria	12
At the Races, Alexandria	16
A Company Bivouac in a Wadi	20
The Mess at Slag Heap	28
Throat Inspection of " Y " Company by Captain A. B. Sloan, R.A.M.C.	32
Church Parade at Slag Heap	36
Baby Camel, three days old	44
A Sand Sledge at El Arish	48
Caterpillars dragging Heavy Guns along the Shore between Gaza and Askalon, 8th Nov. 1917	64
Bringing in the Wounded on Cacolets, Wadi Hesi	68
At the Orange Grove near Wadi Hesi	76
Battalion Headquarters beside the Well at Esdud (Ashdod)	80
A Native House at Beshshit	82
Lieut. Col. J. M. Findlay, reading the proclamation at Ekron	84
Bringing up the Guns into the Hills	94
Kubeibeh (Emmaus) looking east, with Neby Samwil in the distance	96
Typical Scenery in the Hills	100
Native Dwellings at Beit Anan	108
156 Brigade Column leaving Beit Anan	112
A Bye-way in Sarona	124
Pontoon Bridge across the Auja	128

Turkish Trenches captured on North Bank of the Auja	136
Jerusalem. The City Walls and Mount of Olives from Mount Zion	150
Jerusalem. Mosque of Omar and the Temple Area	154
Garden of Gethsemane	156
Bethlehem. In the Church of the Holy Nativity	160
Pylons at the Temple of Isis. Philae	164
The Great Barrage, near Assouan	168
In the Temple of Ammon at Karnak, Luxor	172
Convoy Carrying the 52nd (Lowland) Division to France	182
H.M.T. "Canberra." The Staff	186

MAPS.

Sketch Map of the Position before Gaza	56
,, ,, showing the advance on Jaffa	116
,, ,, of Environs of Jaffa	144
,, ,, of Vimy District	216
,, ,, of country S.W. of Soissons	232

THE ROAD TO THE FRONT

OVERLAND TO MARSEILLES—A COMPLETE GUIDE TO THE DUTIES OF SHIP'S ADJUTANT—LIFE ON A "TROOPER"—PERQUISITES AT MALTA—ALEXANDRIA—THE CAMPAIGN AGAINST GREASE—TO THE PROMISED LAND VIA KANTARA AND ROMANI—OF THE COMFORTS AND CONVENIENCE OF MILITARY TRAVEL

SIX-THIRTY a.m. is apt to be a chilly and cheerless hour on a dull February day, and the 25th day of that month in 1917 proved no exception at Southampton Docks. Our train from Felixstowe had arrived a few minutes earlier, and I was now sitting with Barrett of the Manchesters on some packing cases, wondering what was going to happen next. Along with our draft of two hundred N.C.O.'s and men of the Norfolk Regiment and two sleepy officers of the Embarkation Staff, we were then the only tenants of the huge shed which formed our temporary quarters, but it was not long until other special trains steamed in and disgorged drafts large and small, selected apparently from almost every regiment in the Army List. Tied up to the dock, outside the shed, was a weird assortment of ships, ranging from the giant "Aquitania," clad in the white vestments of a hospital ship, to the merest tramp, camouflaged in the maddest riot of colouring and design.

After rations and ammunition had been issued to the draft, nothing remained but to wait for further orders. It was not till 5 p.m. that the drafts were led along to the gangway of a cross-channel steamer. It required considerable skill to pack all the troops on board, but this was safely accomplished, and an hour later, when lifebelts had been issued, we moved away from the dock-side into the night. Fortunately, I was not detailed for any specific duty, so after seeing the draft settled down and getting a meal, I turned-in with Barrett in a comfortable two-berth cabin. The night was calm, and by 9 a.m. next morning we had passed inside the boom defences at Havre and steamed up the harbour.

Disembarkation proceeded immediately, and the drafts, comprising in all about 1,500, marched some two miles along the dock road to the Rest Camp. As the special trains for Marseilles were not due to leave until night, some of us went along to the town for lunch, and secured a supply of provisions for the two days' journey. We found, on returning, that of the two special trains required only one would leave that night, the other following in the morning, and that the Norfolk draft was detailed to travel by the first train. It was just dark when we left Havre, and as Barrett and I were the only occupants of a first-class compartment, we travelled in comparative luxury. We skirted Paris by the line which passes close to

THE ROAD TO THE FRONT

Versailles, and after spending two nights and two days in the train, reached Marseilles about 10 p.m. on the 28th.

The moonlight was of extraordinary brilliance as we marched out by the low road to Camp Carcassonne. Here we spent a very chilly night under canvas. The camp was most picturesquely situated on the hillside above the shore road, a part of it being shut off for the use of native Indian troops. In the forenoon of the following day I received a message from the Camp Adjutant stating that I was detailed as Ship's Adjutant, and that I was to proceed to the docks in the early afternoon with the O.C. troops to make arrangements for embarkation in the evening. Now the job of Ship's Adjutant was one that I had been warned at all hazards to avoid, and I felt no gratitude for the appointment. Major J. Liddle, R.F.C., was to be O.C. troops on board, and with him I set out for the docks. Our ship was the "Tunisian," an eight thousand tonner, and we were soon engaged with the Embarkation Officer in making all arrangements for the disposal of the troops on board. In the evening I brought the drafts along from the camp, and by 8 p.m. all were safely on board ship. I was sorry to find that Barrett was not to accompany us further. He had been detailed, before leaving home, as Subaltern with my draft, and on reaching Egypt would naturally have been posted to the 42nd Division. That division, however, was in actual process of returning to France from Egypt when we reached Marseilles, so the luck of the game led Barrett back by train to the North instead of by ship to the East.

Later, at night, the second train from Havre arrived, and the remainder of the ship's company was embarked. Being Adjutant, I secured a very luxurious cabin on the top deck, with arm-chairs, a large table, a private bathroom and a bed. On the morning of the 2nd the troops were allotted the boat stations to which they would go in the event of an alarm, and lifebelts were inspected. There are great disadvantages attached to the job of Ship's Adjutant when the entire ship's company is composed of a large number of small drafts whose officers, being drawn from different regiments, have only seen their drafts for the first time some four days earlier. If, in addition, there happen to be 300 naval ratings on board, with only one officer, the job is still further complicated.

On the evening of the 2nd we left Marseilles escorted by a British sloop. The officers were at dinner when we moved down the harbour, and about half an hour later, when we were coming abreast of Château d'If, someone came to the smoke-room and told us we had been in collision with our escort, and were now making back again for the harbour. We had not been conscious of any violent impact, and believed the tale to be merely the product of someone's distorted sense of humour, until a steward came in and announced that "boat stations" had been ordered. I thought it high time then to find the O.C. troops, and, incidentally, to fumble for the nozzle of my Gieve waistcoat.

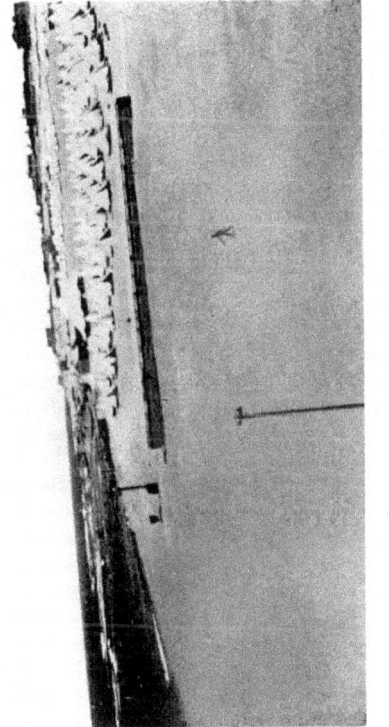

BASE DEPOT AT MUSTAPHA, NEAR ALEXANDRIA

THE ROAD TO THE FRONT

From the upper deck a glance showed that we were certainly making, with all speed, for the harbour, and that the ship was already well down by the bows. All the arrangements in event of an alarm had worked well, and within a few minutes the troops were at their stations. It was an anxious quarter of an hour, and there was considerable relief when the Skipper eventually brought the ship alongside one of the docks, with her nose resting well up on the mud. Our escort had struck us a slanting blow and holed us near the bows, with the result that the forward compartment, in which 300 men were quartered, was completely flooded to the top of the companion. Many of the men had been asleep when the accident occurred, but all were roused in time to prevent loss of life. However, all their rifles, equipment, and much of their clothing were now submerged, and the Ship's Quartermaster was kept busy issuing additional blankets and arranging accommodation for the homeless drafts. Fortunately the forward bulkheads had held firm.

Early next morning collision mats were fixed in position, and the pumps got to work, with the result that in twelve hours the forward compartments were clear of water. Meanwhile we had become an object of the greatest interest to all conditions of naval transport officers and embarkation officers, and I was informed that the troops on board would be transferred early on the morning of the 4th to the "Transylvania," a new Cunard-Anchor boat of 17,000 tons, which was lying off in the stream. Transhipment had to be completed by 9 a.m., and I was kept fully employed with the details and general arrangements. In addition, new clothing, boots, etc., had to be procured to take the place of garments lost or destroyed owing to the accident, and the salving of arms, ammunition and equipment was taken in hand. At 6 a.m. on the morning of the 4th transhipment began, and by 9 a.m. all the military drafts and naval ratings were on board the "Transylvania," and a few hours later we pulled out into the stream and hitched up to a buoy. The complement of our new ship was 3,000 troops, and as our present company numbered only 1,500, we were to wait a few more days until two other trainloads of troops should reach Marseilles and join the ship.

By the next day I found myself called upon to make arrangements for transferring the cargo from the "Tunisian" to the "Transylvania," and I became so immersed in affairs of the sea that I almost expected to find bell-mouthed trousers and a sailor hat sprouting at my extremities. Once or twice I managed to go ashore in the evenings, and enjoyed some excellent dinners at the Bristol with Captain O'Brien of the Gurkhas. On the evening of the 9th the other trains arrived, and our full complement was made up. These troops were likewise composed of small drafts, one party consisting of 400 leave details, drawn from nearly every unit in the E.E.F., with no officer in charge. Fortunately by this time I had a week's experience in hand, and was able to appreciate the humours of the situation. Our accident had certainly taught me the necessity of making the minutest arrangements for all eventualities, in addition to the regular routine of the ship and the discipline of the troops.

There are some thirty-five pages of King's Regulations devoted to the subject of the Movement of Troops by Sea, but these thirty-five pages were penned for use during the Indian trooping season in the piping and leisurely days of peace, before the game of "hide and seek" with enemy submarines had become a popular pastime. Part of my job was to modernise these thirty-five pages and, with many additions and more deletions, to render them applicable and suitable to present conditions. I found, however, that by giving strict attention to the following rules the business became much more pleasant and simple :

1. Get on the right side of the Naval Transport Officer and the Embarkation Officer. It should be noted that they are fairly sure to consider each other as hopelessly incapable dug-outs, and both are possibly correct.
2. Find out the brand of cocktail which appeals to their taste.
3. If the Embarkation Officer happens to be a retired Indian Army officer, study the state of his liver.
4. Make sure that the best, or second best, cabin on the ship is placed at your disposal.
5. Find out the peculiarities of the O.C. troops, and act accordingly.

6. Get the ship's Chief Officer well on your side. He can give you all kinds of help, and has always a comfortable cabin in which you can hide at times from the O.C. troops.

7. Don't accept more than half the offers of hospitality you may receive in the smoke-room, otherwise work after lunch may become wearisome.

8. Remember that such words as "right" and "left" when applied to the ship are temporarily taboo, and replies to all questions should be couched in thoroughly nautical language. This has a great moral effect.

And last and most important—

9. Appoint a thoroughly efficient and hard-working Assistant Adjutant.

On 9th March we finally left the docks, and after waiting for some hours in the little bay just to the west of the harbour, the voyage started.

We were escorted by two British destroyers, which kept their stations on either bow or scurried off in front on a wild zig-zag course with seething tracks of foam trailed out astern. The davit guards were in position beside the ship's boats on the upper deck, the ammunition party lay ready by the 4.7 inch gun on the poop, and the daily ship's inspection was safely over. The latter is almost the principal event in the day's routine at sea. All the troops are on parade at their stations, and the fatigue and sanitary parties have completed their work in the different messes, sleeping quarters

THE ROAD TO THE FRONT

and other intimate parts of the ship's interior. Then at a given hour a perspiring party of officers led by the O.C. troops pursues the Skipper up and down narrow ladders into the bowels of the ship with noses at the alert to track down any lurking smell, and eyes skinned to detect even so much as a stray tea leaf still clinging affectionately to the inside of a kettle already passed as clean by the N.C.O. on duty. Occasionally we catch up sufficiently on the Skipper to receive the backwash of a string of grumbles, but usually he is well ahead, with the pack strung out behind in full cry. After a long and stern chase the after companion disgorges us, faint yet pursuing, somewhere near the poop, and the inspection of the troops begins. A signal by whistle eventually dismisses the parade, and the crow of the cocktail calls the officers to the smoke-room.

The course followed by troop ships is constantly varied, and the naval authorities had decreed for us a route which led us along the Riviera coast and provided wonderful views of the blue hills of Italy, with the little white villages sprawling on the slopes high above the sea. The evening of the 11th found us nearing the Straits of Messina, and I heard on the quiet that an enemy submarine had been reported by wireless twenty miles astern, following the same track. Just before 5 p.m. we passed through the Straits and along the coast of Sicily. The moon shone with a wonderful brilliance, which tipped the water with shimmering magic, but no doubt added considerably to the anxiety of the Officer of the Watch. At normal steaming it would have been possible to reach Malta at early morning, but entrance to the harbour at Valetta was not permitted till after 9 a.m., by which time the minesweepers' work in the passage outside the harbour would be finished, and the "All Clear" signalled. So it became necessary to waste time, either by reducing speed or by making a detour, in order that the ship should not make harbour until the appointed hour. The process of wasting time amid waters which are the happy hunting-ground of submarines is not the most desirable form of loafing.

We hoped to have at least one day at Valetta, but when the Skipper had returned from his visit to naval headquarters we were told that we must take the road again in the afternoon, and that shore leave was therefore impossible. Here I met with one of the few perquisites pertaining to the office of Ship's Adjutant. The O.C. troops was going ashore on some rather nebulous duty, and I was ordered to accompany him in one of the ship's boats. On reaching the landing-stage we ascended by elevator to the town itself, which stands high on the rocks above the harbour, and then set out at once to fulfil the difficult duty which brought us ashore. This seemed to consist mainly of a short reconnaissance of the town made from among the cushions on the back seat of a two-horse garry. First a small selection of lace had to be purchased, parcelled, addressed for home, and left in the care of the postal authorities. Then we drove down the cobbled street, and stopped at the entrance to the Church of St. John. It is certainly a stately

THE ROAD TO THE FRONT

and dignified home for the knights of that ancient Order, and apart from its beauty is highly endowed with historical interest. Thereafter we clattered down a long narrow street, to find at the end of it a little chapel of morbid personality and freakish decoration. For here was nothing but countless rows of human skulls grinning down from the walls and arches, worked here and there into gruesome patterns edged with cross-bones. It was a dismal, chilly spot, and the cheer and warmth of the afternoon sun brought us quickly back to the street. Then, to complete the reconnaissance, we sipped a cup of coffee outside a café in the Square opposite Government House before setting our course once more for the harbour. The view of the harbour from the heights above was undoubtedly the finest thing which Valetta could show. The outlet to the sea is so small as almost to escape notice, and the harbour itself is fringed at one point with docks, naval workshops, a hospital, and all the paraphernalia of the Senior Service ; while at another are the buildings and jetties of the steamship companies. Moored to buoys were hospital ships, a light cruiser, a small fleet of minesweepers, and a pack of destroyers with steam up and straining like hounds on the leash.

By 5 p.m. the "Transylvania" had passed out of the Harbour with the two French destroyers, which had relieved our previous escort, bustling on ahead. The weather was fine, and life on board settled down again to the daily routine. Our course led along toward Crete before turning south, and by noon on 16th March we had passed down the long line of buoys which act as sign-posts, and had safely entered Alexandria Harbour. We were at once boarded by a bevy of naval, medical and military officers, and I was soon in the midst of detailed arrangements for disembarkation. Fortunately this was not to take place till the morning, and I was able, meantime, to keep the Military Landing Officer fairly well at bay with stacks of nominal rolls and countless army forms. The work of the next day started early, but by 3 p.m. all the officers and drafts had been sorted out, shepherded ashore, and started off with their rations to the respective camps. The day was very warm, and being constantly on the move, I was conscious of the loss of much tissue, in addition to my voice. Dinner at the Majestic was a cheerful affair, after which Major Liddle and I returned to sleep on board, and with the troops all now ashore, we enjoyed an atmosphere freed from responsibilities.

On the afternoon of the 18th March I reported to one of the Infantry Base Depots at Mustapha, a suburb on the coast about six miles east of Alexandria. The Norfolk draft had gone to a different depot, but I was put in charge of some other drafts which had also come on the "Transylvania," and in this job had the assistance of Willie Cumming and Sillars.

Even an Infantry Base Depot is at times disturbed by the really important issues of war, and some little time previously a crisis had occurred when a certain Staff Officer of ferocious mien, due

RACES AT THE SPORTING CLUB, ALEXANDRIA

THE ROAD TO THE FRONT

probably to a slightly distended liver, had inspected a draft and discovered signs of grease lurking on the tunic collars of some of the men. And so at this particular period a strenuous campaign was in full swing with the object of permanently eliminating any suggestion of all such offending stains. During the next fortnight I had therefore to become a laundry expert, and batches of men were marched daily to the ablution houses in which with brushes, soap and water they could strive to remove the damning evidence of their honest sweat. The results of the treatment produced temporary improvement, but Nature is a sturdy antagonist, and in a country of hot suns, high collars, and route marches, no panacea for the trouble was discovered. In the course of time the Great Staff Officer Himself came to inspect our drafts, and the air was heavy with fear and forebodings. A minute examination of the backs of tunic collars was the principal item in the ceremony, and he eventually left the Parade Ground quite satisfied because his hawk-like eye had in a few cases still succeeded in detecting lingering signs of the epidemic.

Apart from the laundry business and a long series of kit inspections and inoculation parades, there were many bright spots during the time at Mustapha, and very frequently in the afternoons we took tea and listened to the band on the shady lawn of the Sporting Club, or went into Alexandria to dine at one of the clubs whose doors stood hospitably open to officers. In the day's agenda too was often found a glass of iced coffee with whipped cream at Groppi's. I spent one very interesting day with the Royal Flying Corps at Aboukir, and visited with Major Liddle the ruins of ancient Canopus.

We were glad, however, when, on the 28th March, we got orders that our drafts would entrain on the following night for Kantara. And so on the 29th we again took the road and left Mustapha by a train about 8 p.m. I found myself in command, but my duties seemed to include nothing more serious than simply to occupy the first-class compartment which was at my disposal. We reached Kantara at 5 a.m. on the 30th, and after seeing all the drafts off to their respective Rest Camps, I had a cup of tea with a hospitable R.T.O. in a railway carriage, which was fitted out with much comfort as his living quarters. Then crossing the Canal by the swing bridge, I came to the Rest Camp near the terminus of the Military Railway. Kantara as the base of the Army in the desert was a large town of marquees, tents and rush-huts planted down on the deep desert sand, and here and there by the side of its roads were large R.E. dumps, supply and ordnance stores, motor transport parks, and the sheds of the Railway Operating Department.

We left Kantara on the 31st March at 3 a.m., in accordance with the peculiar regulation of military travel, which seems to decree that your train must start or reach its destination in the smallest hours of the morning. The train was composed of open trucks, and was bound for Romani. The journey was very cold, but it did not last long, for at

THE ROAD TO THE FRONT

4.30 a.m. we reached our destination, and at the station I finally handed over the drafts belonging to the other divisions, and set out with a guide and our own drafts for the 52nd Divisional Details Camp. The marquees and tents of the camp lay about a quarter of a mile from the station, on a gentle slope of fine clean sand, and after arranging for the drafts, I secured a few hours' sleep in the Officers' Mess marquee.

It was a great relief to be at last with our own Division, and the days at Romani leave behind a very happy memory. The Camp itself was under the genial rule of Major Agnew of the 5th A. & S.H., while the 156 Brigade Company fell under the supervision of James Austin of the 7th Scottish Rifles. Here I found a large draft for the 8th Scottish Rifles under Bathgate, which had arrived by an earlier transport, but had been quarantined at a little distance outside the Camp on account of some infectious trouble. It was not free to proceed up the line for another week, and during that time it was placed under my charge. On one day we marched over to the coast at Mohammediya to bathe, and on another we plodded through the deep, soft sand to Katib-Ganet, a high conical sand dune like a miniature Matterhorn, which stands up as a landmark about two and a half miles distant. From the Signal Station at the top of the hill we were able to obtain a fine view of Wellington Ridge and the country over which the Battle of Romani had been fought in August, 1916.

On the 4th April while we were at lunch in the

Mess an enemy plane flew low over the Station and the Camp. The three bombs which were dropped with the apparent intention of destroying the water tanks near the Station, fortunately missed their mark, and we were exceedingly lucky in having no casualties from the machine gun fire which was then opened on our Camp.

The Officers' Mess was the proud possessor of a piano, most of the notes of which were still in commission, and of several officers who were excellent performers, and the evenings were usually filled in with a musical symposium or bridge.

For some days rumours of the first and indecisive engagement at Gaza had been filtering down the line, and it seemed apparent that this could only be the prelude to something bigger. These expectations further developed when orders arrived for all drafts to proceed forthwith to join their Battalions. The majority of the drafts left Romani on the 7th April, but the 156 Brigade drafts were among the last to go, and I was not in the least surprised to hear that our train was due to leave the station at the convenient hour of 3.30 a.m. on the 8th. I took the drafts to the station at 9 p.m. on the previous night, and the men slept on the soft sand near by until the train arrived. When it steamed in, each truck seemed already to be piled high with rations, coal, or other material, but eventually the three hundred men of the drafts were all safely stowed away among the ration boxes, to which they clung like limpets. Bathgate and I could find nothing better for ourselves than a truck filled with small stones which was near the engine.

W. S. SCOTT.   E. R. B.

AT THE RACES, ALEXANDRIA.

When the train had started we spread out our valises on the top of the stones, and managed to secure a comparatively comfortable bed. Unfortunately our truck had been selected by necessity and not as the result of tactical foresight, and owing to our close proximity to the engine we repeatedly found our blankets smouldering, due to their contact with the sparks, which showered upon us. Our bodies also became deeply ingrained with black coal dust. It was rather a relief next forenoon when the engine broke down at Tilul, for before another arrived, we had time for a wash and a transfer of our quarters to the brake van. Although it was a weary journey, it was interesting to see the vast stretch of desert on all hands ; to realise that our troops had plodded every foot of the way through the wastes of sand, and to see by the side of the railway the pipe-line which carried its stream of Nile water to within reach of the front line. We had tea in the Officers' Rest Tent at El Arish, and reached Rafa at 9.30 p.m. Our progress had become so leisurely that we almost despaired of ever reaching our destination, and, as a matter of fact, we were all asleep when we jolted to a standstill at the chilly hour of 5 a.m. on the 9th April, and found ourselves at Deir El Belah.

IN FRONT OF GAZA

THE SECOND BATTLE OF GAZA : APRIL, 1917—CONSOLIDATION—HOW TO BUILD A TANK—SLAG HEAP—A NEW RECIPE FOR SCONES—THE USE OF THE BAYONET IN WAR—LEAVE—THE PLEASURES OF PATROLLING—THE COST OF POPULARITY—THE COMPLETE METHOD OF RATIONING AN INFANTRY BRIGADE—INTENSIVE TRAINING—SHEIKH AJLIN—SOME PREPARATIONS FOR BATTLE—A SCANDAL—THE THIRD BATTLE OF GAZA : NOVEMBER, 1917—CHITS.

AFTER three hours' rest the men had breakfast, and Bathgate and I got some tea from the kitchen of the Y.M.C.A. near the station. Guides had arrived from the battalions, and after handing over the drafts for the other units, we set off for our own Headquarters. We found the Battalion bivouacked about a mile and a half away, and when I had reported our arrival the Colonel inspected the draft. They were really a first-rate lot of men, and probably the best draft which had ever reached the Battalion. Personally I was more than glad to be with my own people again. In due course I was posted to "Y" Company, and was glad to find that Curtis, who came up with the draft, was

IN FRONT OF GAZA

appointed Company Sergeant-Major. The officers of the Company whom I knew were Allan Rogers, Robb Cree, and Thom ; the others I had not met before.

At this time preparations were in full swing for the second attack on Gaza, and I spent as much time as possible in making myself acquainted with the Company. The railway station at Deir-el-Belah (familiarly known by the troops as "Dear Old Bella") is in the middle of a vast plain, the whole expanse of which seemed to be alive with field hospitals, bivouacs and dumps. Never-ending columns of camels and horse transport were moving to and fro with rations or to the watering-places near the beach, leaving behind them long trails of dust. Here and there a small red pennant showed the Headquarters of a Brigade or Division.

Two days later I accompanied the Colonel and one or two others on a reconnaissance of the positions across the Wadi Ghuzze. It was a wonderfully clear day, and I was very glad to get an idea of the country. The distance to the wadi was about a couple of miles, and on the way we passed through the outposts, which were held at that time by the H.L.I. Brigade. The wadi itself is a broad dry watercourse with lofty banks, rising in places to a height of forty feet, and a sandy bed. While it is dry during the greater part of the year, it becomes a rushing torrent during the rainy season.

At one point we dismounted behind a little rise, from which a very fine view was obtained. From there I had my first sight of Tel-el-Ajjul, Red

House, Burjaliye, Sheikh Nebhan, Dorset House, and many other landmarks, which later on became very intimate friends. Away in front was the Promised Land, looking very pretty and green, with clumps of poppies and spring flowers lending touches of colour. A few miles ahead, and near the shore, the white roofs of Gaza, with its mosque and minaret, could be plainly seen. Then we carried on across the wadi, and, leaving the horses again with the grooms, we watched the skirmishing lines of the 6th H.L.I. clearing some Turks from the wooded enclosure at Burjaliye. After reconnoitering the ground round Dorset House—where it was then expected the Battalion would lie during the preliminary stage of the battle—we made our way back to Belah. It was an intensely interesting day, and called for more rough-riding on my part than I was almost prepared to display. Practice attacks, inspections of equipment, etc., filled in the days.

On the 14th April I found myself Divisional Field Officer, and spent most of the day and bits of the night riding round the guards, wells, watering-places, etc. I also made my first inspection of a Tank.

About this time orders were received as to the composition of the nucleus to be left behind when the engagement began, and I found myself ordered to take charge of the Battalion Details. It was arranged therefore that Allan Rogers should take " Y " Company, and afterwards he carried on in command.

On Sunday, 15th April, just as the men were

A COMPANY BIVOUAC IN A WADI.

IN FRONT OF GAZA

falling in for Church Parade, three shells from a long-range gun landed in or near the camp. The first claimed several casualties, among them being Scotland, one of the officers of "Y" Company, who was wounded in the head. On the morning of the 16th, Operation Orders having been received, the Colonel held a final " pow-wow " with all the officers and arrangements were completed. That night the Battalion marched off to its forward area, two companies under Dai Carson being detached as artillery escort. I hardly felt qualified to hold any very definite views regarding the plan of the battle, but it seemed to me broadly as though the total frontage of the attack had simply been divided more or less equally among the available divisions ; that the attack—a frontal one—was aimed at the strongest point in the enemy defences, and that there was little to be recognised in the way of strategy or finesse. During the next two days I was fully occupied moving the battalion dump and the nucleus to the Divisional Area at Piccadilly Circus, about a mile nearer the wadi.

On the 19th the bombardment of the enemy position both from our artillery and from the fleet was very heavy, but hardly as intense as I had expected. From a hill near the dump I watched the shells bursting in and around Gaza, which was almost hidden under the heavy pall of smoke. Then a few casualties began to arrive at the Field Ambulance near Piccadilly Circus, and I posted a man there to bring me news of those who passed through and find out if we could do anything to help them. I saw Archie M'Laren and Westland, and got their valises over in time to accompany them down the line. Fortunately neither was seriously wounded. Along with the wounded came down the wonderful assortment of rumours which hatch and float about in great profusion in the area behind every engagement. At one time our men were carrying all before them, and complete victory was only a question of an hour or two. A few minutes later they were being pressed back, casualties were enormous, and the Colonel and most of the officers killed. Fortunately none of these reports was believed, and a little later a chit reached me from the Battalion which told me something between these extremes; that the Battalion had done fine work, but that the line was held up and casualties fairly heavy. Then came requests for details to be sent up from the nucleus, and pathetic appeals for such important things as mess stores and beer.

On the following afternoon I rode over with Padre Wilson to attend the funeral of one of our men, the burial ground being a large enclosure surrounded by a cactus hedge. On Sunday, 22nd, I got orders to move everything up to the Battalion, and in the evening sent off M'Combie with forty-three camels and about two-thirds of the contents of the dump. On the forenoon of the 23rd thirty-four additional camels were sent to me, and by 3 p.m. the dump was cleared and we were loaded up and *en route*.

The net result of the battle now concluded was a general advance of some three miles, which

IN FRONT OF GAZA

brought the defences of Gaza within effective striking distance.

We reached the Battalion at 6 p.m., just as it was getting dark, and found it lying in a little wadi below the conical hill called Tel-el-Ahmar, and about half a mile behind Mansura Ridge. Our Battalion, which had apparently suffered more heavily in casualties than the others in the Brigade, was in reserve, and very fully employed with night working parties. The ground between Tel-el-Ahmar and the Ridge is a great basin flanked by rising ground. Near us was a very active field battery, which attracted to itself, and to us, unpleasant attentions from the Turkish gunners. At this particular battery we noticed a horse standing tethered near the guns, and this animal must certainly have been endowed with a most placid disposition. Occasionally the enemy shelling became so heavy that the men had to leave the guns and take cover, but on each occasion when the smoke cleared away the horse was still there safe and sound and apparently quite unconcerned. Some humourist who helps to make the maps christened this area " Sleepy Hollow."

Our line ran about 500 yards in front of the Ridge, and from dark to dawn we were kept busy with parties working in reliefs on the front and support lines. From the 24th to the 26th I had my first experience of a "Khamseen." This takes the form of a strong south wind from the desert, which blows in hot blasts and carries with it thick clouds of dust and sand. The heat was grilling (temperature 110 degrees in the shade), and left the nose and mouth dry and parched and the body limp. Drinks are of little avail while the Khamseen blows, for they are as hot as the wind itself, and relief only comes at night or when the Khamseen blows itself out, usually on the third day.

On the 28th April the Battalion was ordered to garrison a number of redoubts which had been started as a second defensive line. At dusk "Y" Company moved to No. 5 Redoubt, beside Tel-el-Ahmar, and Battalion Headquarters back to a little wadi near Burjaliye. The trenches in the redoubt had been started by the 155 Brigade, but were in a very unfinished state and in parts only a foot or so deep. This necessitated strenuous work all night, and also by day on parts which were not exposed to view. In a few days we managed to effect great improvements, and Allan Rogers and I completed a small tee-shaped dug-out. Robb Cree, who had been detached during the battle for duty with the 53rd Division, rejoined us here, and on occasional visits from Steven Bilsland, who was with "Z" Company in the neighbouring redoubt, we managed an afternoon rubber of bridge. The vicinity of these redoubts became a favourite landing ground for 5.9's, and it requires more than all the concentration to be obtained from the little grey books of Pelmanism to keep attention fixed firmly on the game when it is played in an uncovered dug-out with shells bursting in the near vicinity.

On Sunday, 6th May, we received orders to move again, and I spent the forenoon as a member of my first Field General Court Martial. It was

IN FRONT OF GAZA

held in a sand-bagged dug-out at the Headquarters of the 4th Royal Scots, who were holding a sector of the front line. We packed up in the afternoon, and prepared to move whenever it was dusk. Turkish aeroplanes had been very busy with night bombing raids, and, as it was brilliant moonlight, we hoped they might take a rest on this particular night. When making our dug-out we had managed to acquire two sheets of corrugated iron, which at that time was more precious than rubies, and we determined, if possible, to take them with us to our next little home. The only method of transit was by camel, and loading sheets of corrugated iron on a camel is at best a ticklish business. It becomes more difficult when the camel shows a distinct disinclination to lend itself to the enterprise. Just as we were getting the load securely fixed the camel would try to rise, and the whole load would fall off with a terrific jangle, which increased the camel's nervousness. However, after many failures we got the load firmly adjusted, and the beast got on to its feet, looking more like an improved pattern of Tank than a decent camel. Incidentally, if it moved its head suddenly to one side or the other it ran a fair risk of beheading itself on the sharp edge of the sheets which stuck out in front. However, we were now ready to start, and just as we got well into the open three enemy planes, whose bombs we had heard fall somewhere near Belah, came back and passed directly over us. The moonlight was very bright, and as they opened up with their machine guns while just over our heads, we could hardly hope we had escaped detection. However, they passed on, and we had no casualties. There are few things so unpleasant as wandering about with a string of camels when under fire. We had no further adventure, and reached our new home at Slag Heap two hours later. Slag Heap was a big redoubt just to the west of Kurd Hill and about one-and-a-half miles nearer the sea than our previous quarters. It was garrisoned by "X" and "Y" Companies, and from its fire trenches in the afternoon light a splendid view of Gaza and its gardens could be obtained.

We spent a very pleasant and, on the whole, an uneventful time at Slag Heap during the next four weeks. The garrison was ample for the usual duties, and daily work parties on the trenches at Queen's Hill or for burying signal cable, became the routine. Battalion Headquarters were at El Sire, threequarters of a mile farther back, and we looked forward to the daily visit of Doctor Sloan, who brought the day's budget of rumours and news of the outside world. At this time there was an epidemic of sore throats among the men, and an order went forth that daily gargling was to take place. It was a quaint sight to see the company on parade, each man with his head well back, while the air was filled with the concentrated noise of the gurgling of a thousand gasogenes, all operating in different keys.

Flies also became a perfect plague, and mosquito netting an absolute essential. This fly was not the homely animal which fled at the word "shoo," but a more adventurous and persistent

IN FRONT OF GAZA

type, which got into everything and loved to settle on your nose or ears, or crawl up and down your fork at meals, having literally to be pushed off before consenting to retire. Very efficient sanitary arrangements were necessary to cope with the fly danger, and the sun was never too hot to keep the Doctor from his daily inspection of latrines, grease traps and cookhouses. Occasionally a wandering scorpion visited our dugout at night, and one of the men who was using his pack as a pillow found a three-foot long snake contentedly coiled up inside it. "Quick Dick," an 18-pounder battery not far from us, disturbed our sleep with spasms of night firing, but in spite of all, these days were not unpleasant, and with Allan Rogers, "Bombs" Westland and Robb Cree available we had many good rubbers of bridge in our little canvas-covered mess behind the hill.

Our Officers' Mess cook at this time had in pre-war days plied the trade of a baker, and having received an issue of flour as part of our ration, we suggested a display of his prowess in manufacturing scones for afternoon tea. An apparently insuperable difficulty arose owing to the absence of any baking powder with which to "raise" the scones, until Robb Cree, in a wave of extraordinary resourcefulness, suggested Eno's fruit salts as a substitute. The resulting scones were quite astonishing in their effects and a wonderful advertisement to the skill of the cook coupled with Messrs. Eno.

At this time our Flying Corps exhibited great activity. During parts of each day planes cruised over the Turkish positions taking photographs, and the sky was constantly dotted with the bursts of shrapnel and H.E. from enemy "Archies." The sturdy contempt of these details shown by our pilots and observers certainly won our admiration, but an unpleasant feature of these exhibitions was the steady stream of shrapnel and bits of shell-case which rained down on the locality of Slag Heap.

It was while we were here that poor Bowen was killed. He was in his shack at Battalion Headquarters when a Turkish anti-aircraft shell, failing to explode in the air, burst on contact, and a piece of shell penetrated the shack. The Battalion lost a grand quarter-master and a good friend and comrade. While at El Sire, Dulieu went home on leave and Innes took on the work of Adjutant.

By this time the days had become very hot, and even in the morning it was necessary to wear a sun-helmet when engaged in the daily ablutions in half a canvas bucket of water, referred to out of courtesy as a bath. At El Sire Dick Coulson rejoined the Battalion from hospital. We had many cheerful little dinner parties, and were quite sorry when, on the night of 12/13th June, we were relieved by the 10th London Battalion, and moved over to a reserve area at Wadi Laban, one of the small tributary wadis of the Nukhabir, and some four miles further inland from Slag Heap.

The night march to our new quarters was no easy one. The night was dark, and our way across country was intersected at different angles by

THE MESS AT SLAG HEAP

numerous wadis. Allan Rogers exhibited considerable skill in keeping correct direction.

Owing to the kindness of a friendly R.E. officer we were able to build a very imposing Officers' Mess. Allan Rogers and I shared a roomy shack cut into the reverse slope of a mound, and as usual we slept in our valises on the ground. It was here that I had my first and only experience in wielding the bayonet against an enemy. On one particular night we were wakened by sand and earth falling on our pillows (or what did duty as pillows) from the ledge above our heads. From experience we knew that this meant only one thing, and that was that a mouse, a scorpion, or a tarantula was engaged on a night patrol above us. The "shoo" which would have scared a mouse was ineffective, for the sand and earth continued to fall; so I picked up my electric torch and got up to reconnoitre. After a little hunt the beam fell on a nasty-looking scorpion just above my bed. The scorpion then proceeded to tumble down on to my pillow, which action made me very unhappy. However, plucking up my courage and my bayonet at the same moment, I dealt it the death blow, and with the exception of a nasty stain on my valise, we were none the worse. We had no sooner settled down again to sleep when further assortments of earth and sand began to trickle down on us, and, like good soldiers, in a trice we became all alert. Again I reached for my torch, and with the aid of a stick began a grand sweep of the ledge above, starting from my own side of the shack, so that—as Rogers was quick to point out—any animal that my stick might encounter would assuredly fall on his bed. I, of course, scorned any ulterior motive of that sort, and, as a matter of fact, when something did fall, it fell directly between our valises. On inspection we found it to be a tarantula of unpleasantly generous proportions. Again the death blow was dealt, and we sank once more exhausted to our slumbers.

At this time Doctor A. B. Sloan, who had worked himself to a shadow during the heat of the past two months, took ill and was evacuated to hospital. It was obvious that he needed a long rest, and the Battalion said good-bye to him with the keenest regret. He had been with the Battalion since mobilisation in 1914, and was certainly the doyen of regimental M.O.'s.

During our stay in the territory of the Laban tribe we did some quite strenuous training, and, among other things, embarked on a series of battalion drills. These are not unpleasant when performed on a barrack square, but when they take place on ground which is four inches deep in soft dust they are apt to lose some of their attractiveness, particularly if you yourself form one of the crowd of foot-sloggers. So bad was the dust that when the Battalion practised wheeling in mass it was often impossible even to discern the outline of the company on our immediate flank, and much time was subsequently spent in removing the dust from our perspiring persons. On one day the whole Brigade engaged in a very interesting and instructive practice attack on a series of trenches and a strong-point. New methods of organisation

IN FRONT OF GAZA

and procedure were used for the first time, and it seemed as though all the "Brass Hats" in Palestine had come to see the performance.

While here the Battalion managed to carry through some very successful sports, at which Colonel Peebles—who was acting Brigade Commander at the time—presented the prizes. The mule races and other mounted events were a great feature.

By the 2nd July my turn for Egyptian leave had arrived, and I set out with Scott for Alexandria. We spent seven excellent days at the "Majestic," living well and making the fullest use of our bath. We bathed at Stanley Bay, dined and wined in the airy dining-room of the Union Club or on the balcony of the Sultan Hussein above the Bourse, looking down on the great Square. We attended the races at the Sporting Club, and had our first flight in an aeroplane from Aboukir, flying above the ruins of ancient Canopus and out over the blue waters of the bay.

On the 9th July we left Alexandria again, and rejoined the Battalion in the Skeikh Abbas Apex on the following evening. On my return I found that Willie Law had been appointed D.A.A.G. to a new division, that Bruce Allan was now Staff Captain, and that Steven Bilsland had been taken to Brigade Headquarters as his assistant.

The Sheikh Abbas Apex formed the eastern salient of our line before it bent back toward Goliath Ridge and the redoubts in the Mendur locality. The ridge, which rises abruptly to a height of sixty feet and confines the salient like a wall to the north and east, is really an eastern continuation of the Mansura Ridge, and formed our defensive line. From the crest of the ridge toward the north the ground falls gradually away, and across the face of the forward slope lay our fire and support trenches. The ground shut in by the ridge to the south is fairly level, and hard up against the face, like a huge rabbit warren, were the dug-outs of Battalion and Company Headquarters. From our front trenches the ground sloped gently down for some four hundred yards to the Wadi Endless, which ran along roughly parallel to our line. On the other side of the wadi the ground rose again in a gradual slope for nearly a mile, till it reached the Turkish wire in front of Tank Redoubt and its attendant systems of trenches. Sticking up like a black beetle in the midst of the Redoubt was one of our Tanks, which had been burned out on the 19th April and marooned there when our line was drawn back to its present position. Away to our left bristled the Turkish defences on Ali-el-Muntar, the hill on the landward side of Gaza to which Samson is said to have carried the gates.

Under the circumstances in which we lived for the next few weeks there was very little time to spare in searching for, or even noticing, the picturesque, but for all that, the view from our front-line trenches in the early morning or evening light, looking away past the Turkish line and the Beersheba road to the southern spurs of the Judean hills, is the pleasantest memory of a very wearing four weeks.

THROAT INSPECTION OF "Y" COMPANY BY CAPT. A. B. SLOAN, R.A.M.C.

IN FRONT OF GAZA

The Turkish garrison opposite us was said to be their crack regiment, and it was considered necessary that their activities should be kept well in check and that we should quickly secure and retain an undoubted control of No Man's Land. This process entailed constant night patrols, a form of entertainment which seemed to be particularly adapted to the slim characteristics of the wily Turk. Now patrolling, to my mind, is undoubtedly one of the poorer forms of sport. It is a sort of combination of Hide and Seek and Blind Man's Buff, and when played in the dark over a square mile of country with bombs and bayonets is apt to become a distinctly dangerous pastime. To give the Turk his due, he was both very skilful and daring ; and to begin with, his object seemed to be to get down into the Wadi Endless immediately it became dark and lie up for our patrols as they left our lines. On at least three occasions I took out patrols when we knew that the Turk was already waiting on the prowl out in front, but although the patrol orders were varied nightly in the hope of a successful meeting, only on one occasion did a patrol from the Battalion have a real collision with the enemy.

After creeping out one night through our wire, with fifteen men, we made our way across the wadi to a point where a path led down from the Turkish side, and there I placed the men with a view to scuppering any enemy patrol that might approach. My orders were to wait there till dawn. The ground where we were had been ploughed at some earlier time, and we lay for four hours in the crops between the furrows. One would have thought that under the circumstances every nerve would be tense and alert, but the sound of an occasional snore quickly taught me that part of my job was actually to keep the men from falling asleep. Anyone who has been in charge of a patrol, moving at some distance from his own wire, knows the responsibility and difficulty attached to keeping direction in the dark and the relief when he returns and strikes the right gap in the wire. In these days compasses were our constant companions and Cassiopeia and the Great Bear valued friends.

Probably Ferguson, of "W" Company, had a more intimate knowledge of No Man's Land than anyone else, for he always seemed to be engaged in schemes which entailed spending the night watches more or less on his own, pushing propaganda under the Turkish wire or trying to get our artillery on to enemy patrols or working parties. Enemy artillery fire on our positions was pretty constant, and on the 19th July little M'Leod, an officer of "Z" Company, was killed by the back burst of a whizz-bang which landed on the parados of our fire trenches. He was much missed, for his cheerfulness would have been an asset to any battalion. On the 20th July I was transferred, as Second in Command, to "Z" Company, of which Scott was Skipper while Eric Findlay was in hospital.

About this time it was rather disheartening to notice the superiority of the enemy in the air. This, of course, was not in any way the fault of our airmen but of our machines, which were far

IN FRONT OF GAZA

too slow. We learnt, however, that our inferiority was likely only to be temporary, and was due to some of our ships which were bringing out the fast types of our aeroplanes having fallen victims to enemy submarines in the Mediterranean.

While at the Apex, Innes, who was Acting Adjutant, crocked up and went to hospital, and Dai Carson, who had rejoined from home leave, took over the job until the return of Dulieu. The weather was at its hottest, and even at nights while on duty in the trenches or sleeping on the fire step I wore no jacket, my shirt was open at the neck and my sleeves rolled up. The weather itself was sufficiently trying, but, in addition, we were short of officers, and with constant duties and patrols, it was calculated that the officers got no more than two to three hours' sleep out of the twenty-four. This continual strain was bound to tell on everyone, and I am sure we were all delighted when our tour came to an end and we were relieved by the H.L.I. Brigade on the night of 5/6th August.

On the night of our relief Dai Carson asked one of our men how he had enjoyed his time at the Apex. The man, who in private life had probably plied the peaceful trade of a carter in Townhead, replied that it was all right, " but yon patrollin's no job for a civeelian." I felt the greatest sympathy with his views. " Z " Company was the last to be relieved at the Apex, and we could not reach our new area at Wadi Simeon till 4 a.m. On the following night I got my clothes off and slept in pyjamas—the first time since I had left Alexandria. Then the usual working parties, which are inseparable from all periods of "Rest," started in full swing.

On the night of the 10th/11th August the 156 Brigade moved out to support the Camel Corps in their raid on Sana Redoubt. This entailed taking up a position about one and a half miles in front of our wire, where we lay until our artillery had carried out its bombardment and the Camel Corps had time to do its job. The results of the raid were hardly as great as were expected, and our part in the show was a very peaceful one. On that night Anderson, Carswell, MacDougall and Miller joined the Battalion from home, and I was very glad to see them again, as we had fought together through many bloodless campaigns in Essex and elsewhere.

Then for a few days I was sorely afflicted by one of the minor plagues of Egypt, familiarly known as "Gippy Tummy"; and, added to that, I got a touch of the sun through the roof of my bivouac, which was not sufficiently high to prevent the rays beating down on my head. The result was a splitting headache and internal machinery which refused to answer to the brake in the shape of doses of chlorodine. I was once more regaining my normal health when the Colonel moved me to Battalion Headquarters and handed out to me the jobs of Assistant Adjutant and Intelligence Officer. Dulieu had just returned from leave to his work as Adjutant, and I began to get to grips with such things as Army Forms and the peculiarly dry and pithy type of official correspondence which is common to the Army.

CHURCH PARADE AT SLAG HEAP

IN FRONT OF GAZA

While at the Apex Lyle had joined the Battalion, and having been posted to "Y" Company, he became in the course of time President of the "Y" Company Officers' Mess. Under his strict supervision a complete system of rationing with chits was established, which soon won for him the style and title of "Lord Rhondda." One of the points of the scheme was that the liquid refreshment provided for any guest should be charged to the officer whom the guest had come to visit. This seemed a reasonable plan, but, unfortunately for the complete success of the scheme, its details were whispered abroad, with the unhappy result for the originator that a constant stream of visitors could be seen at all hours wending their way to "Y" Company Mess, all suffering torments of thirst and bent ostentatiously on visiting Lyle. Which leads to the reflection that popularity can sometimes be attained at too high a price!

An experience which fell to my lot here was to act as escort to an officer of another corps who was being tried by General Court Martial. On the day of the trial I had to proceed to the Headquarters of the Battalion where the said officer was under arrest, and escort him to the place of trial and remain with him throughout his ordeal. The trial, which took place in a marquee, was very formal and quite impressive. The Court was composed of some five officers, with a Brigadier-General as president, and among those who took part in the proceedings (though none, needless to say, was in the principal rôle) were John Tulloch, Beaumont Neilson and Jack Findlay. As my job entailed sitting for nearly eight hours on a small-arms ammunition box throughout a very hot day, it will be readily understood by anyone who has rested on the unyielding substance of which these boxes are formed, that my experience was more interesting than comfortable.

Events in the Army have a habit of happening suddenly and unexpectedly, so the following day I found myself *en route* for the Change of Air Camp at El Arish in charge of about forty N.C.O.'s and men from the Battalion. On the way to railhead I spent a night with John Nicholl at the Transport Lines at Sheikh Nebhan, and after dinner in the Brigade Transport Mess I went along to see the nightly issue of rations to the Brigade. Now rations in the first instance are brought up by railway to railhead, and from there are carried forward by the divisional train (not a real, live train, but waggons) to the different Brigade ration dumps. At this point the rations are sorted out for distribution to each unit in the Brigade, and it was this issue at which I was present. It was a pitch-dark night, the only light being from candles standing inside upturned biscuit tins set along a line, each tin with one side knocked out. First the big waggons arrived, and all the different rations were unloaded and placed in piles opposite the candles. First meat, then tea, sugar and milk; then fodder, then meal and rice; then dried fruits, wood-fuel, and so on right down the long list of items. When all had been unloaded the Supply Officer's staff got to work, and butchers were busy hacking carcasses of animals to bring the weights

IN FRONT OF GAZA

correct to the ration strength of each unit. One man, working just beyond the fringe of candle-light, was wielding a huge axe, and Wilks—the Supply Officer—told me he knew the part of the animal he was cutting off would be correct in weight to within half a pound, and that without the use of scales. All the other piles were re-sorted in accordance with a slip placed beside each candle showing the ration strength of each unit in the Brigade. In ten minutes the strings of camels and limber waggons sent from the units wheeled into line in front of the ration piles and the issue began. Another five minutes and it was all over, and when I walked past with Wilks most of the piles had completely vanished along with the camels and limbers. And so the troops, the horses, the camels and the cook-fires were all assured of their food for another day. The darkness made it a weird sight as the camels and waggons emerged from the shadows and dust into the candle light, took their loads and disappeared again. We are really a great army!

The three hours' journey to El Arish was wonderfully comfortable. We travelled in covered trucks which were open at the sides, letting in as much air as possible and giving protection from the sun, and with our valises to lie on we were in comparative luxury. At Khan Yunus and Rafa we saw detachments of our Allies, the French, also some Italian Bersaglieri, and one of our armoured trains.

The organisation of the Change of Air Camp was really a masterpiece. We were met at the station by one of the officers and marched along the shore for about quarter of a mile till we reached the outskirts of the camp. At this point I was told I was relieved of all responsibility for the further care of the men, and directed to the officers' lines. The men then stripped off all their clothes where they stood, and each man was issued with a suit of pyjamas. Their clothes were then put through a process of disinfection, and were returned on the following day. The men lived in tents and messed in large mud brick huts, where rations were plentiful and excellent. Concerts and plays were given nightly, and there were no parades or military work of any kind. The Officers' Mess and anteroom consisted of two large connecting mud huts, the frontage of which was within twenty yards of the water's edge. They were well furnished; the messing was excellent, and such unusual attractions as cocktails, beer, champagne and ice were on tap. I had an iron bedstead with a spring mattress in a double-lined tent behind the mess, and generally was surrounded by every comfort. If any fault could be found with the bathing it was that the water was perhaps a shade too warm.

While there we had a visit from General Allenby, and as I happened to be sitting beside the door through which he entered the Mess, he stopped and asked me a number of questions. I was sorry I had no chance to tell him I was an old Haileyburian. General Allenby had taken over command of the force in June from Sir Archibald Murray, and from the day of his arrival it quickly became apparent that things were moving to some definite object and that someone was pushing from behind. He was certainly a big man in every way, and inspired the greatest confidence. One afternoon I visited a company of the Camel Corps near by. There were some 400 camels, with their pack saddles and equipment dressed in long perfect lines. I also saw four little white baby camels, all less than a week old.

The seven days at El Arish passed quickly, and on 26th August we returned to railhead, and I rejoined the Battalion, which had meantime moved to the Redoubts at Mendur. Mendur itself is a village composed of some three mud huts and a cactus garden; and the Mendur locality comprised a system of works where our line bent right back south-west of the Turkish Ataweeneh Redoubt. Neither on our side nor on the Turkish side was the line at this part a continuous one, and during the three weeks we spent there we were very seldom disturbed. There were nine redoubts in all, and each was self-contained, though all were mutually supporting. While there I found that my own activities were confined to the work of Assistant-Adjutant, and I am certain I must have been a complete nuisance to Dulieu, who took infinite trouble and showed a unique patience in steering me safely through the shoals of Courts Martial and Military Law. An epidemic of sandfly fever kept the doctor busy and carried many officers and men to hospital. The Colonel eventually became a victim, and during his absence Dick Coulson, who had just returned from a Senior Officers' Course at Cairo, took over the command.

One morning about 6 a.m., while it was yet cool, I visited some of the Redoubts with him, and we went out through the wire to inspect an observation post which kept watch on the Turkish positions. On our way back we happened to look over the edge of a steep-sided wadi, and there we found a Turkish soldier sitting on his equipment, looking very unhappy. As we were armed with nothing more deadly than our walking sticks, it was a good thing the Turk had no very warlike intentions. He was, in fact, a very dejected deserter, and only showed signs of cheering up when the escort which I got took him through the lines to a company headquarters where the smell of frizzling bacon greeted him. The social event at Mendur was undoubtedly Archie M'Laren's postponed birthday party, to which John Nicholl and I had the honour of being invited. Barring considerable casualties among the crockery when the table, which was supported by sandbags, unfortunately wilted and collapsed, everything went with a swing. While here, and to my great regret, Dai Carson left us to take up a Staff job with the Labour Corps, the only redeeming feature of his departure being that I fell heir to his very grand and roomy bivouac. The days were still fiery hot, and a prevailing breeze laid a thick layer of dust on everything. A native Indian Battalion came as our guests to Mendur, and our men thoroughly enjoyed the experience of showing them the ropes.

After three weeks at Mendur our wanderings were resumed and the Battalion came to Apsley House, about half a mile on the west side of the

IN FRONT OF GAZA

Wadi Nukhabir. Here we embarked at once on a strenuous three weeks of intensive training. It was quite clear to everyone that our next attack on Gaza could not be at a far distant date, and, with the exception of a break during the heat of the day, work was almost continuous from dawn to dusk. Shortly before this Major-General John Hill had taken over command of the Division from Major-General W. E. B. Smith, and very often by 6.30 a.m. his rotund figure and rubicund face could be seen on horseback approaching the training area.

Since the operations against Gaza in April the Battalion had really had very little chance or opportunity to refit, and every effort was now made to bring the unit to the highest pitch of efficiency. For the officers these days were almost breathless, for, in addition to training with the men, there were daily lectures and demonstrations to be attended. All the same they were good days, and as the whole Brigade was concentrated there was plenty of visiting and entertainment. There was certainly no happier Brigade in the whole British Army than the big family of the 156th, and no officer or man could be in any doubt as to who had achieved this excellent, but by no means universal, state of affairs. Brigadier-General A. H. Leggett, D.S.O., was in command.

The aspect of the country was now very different from the day in April when I first saw it, for now the greenery and flowers were gone, and in their place was one vast drab monotone of dust.

A great deal had been done toward organising the back areas, with the result that the greatest freedom for traffic to all parts of the line had now been secured. Some thirty crossings, each of which was numbered and possessed of a signboard, had been cut through the high banks of the Wadi Ghuzze, and near the sea, where large shallow pools of water lay in the wadi bed, wooden bridges, carrying light railways, had been thrown across. At many points an excellent supply of fresh water was obtained from wells sunk in its sandy bottom. Another factor which greatly simplified movement behind the lines was the network of wire roads which were laid across the sand and stretched out their tentacles in all directions. These wire roads, composed of five widths of rabbit wire laid side by side and bound together at the edges, were a great blessing, as progress on these was much more speedy and less exhausting than on the soft dust and sand. There was a generous supply of signposts, and if in possession of a map you could just as easily find such well-known centres as "Piccadilly Circus," "Regent Park," "Charing Cross," etc., as you could in London.

The Colonel, some other officers and the majority of the men who had gone to hospital from Mendur now began to rejoin, and the Battalion soon regained its usual strength. One evening quite a stir of excitement was caused by a shower of rain, and everyone rushed from his bivouac to watch the drops fall. It was the first rain I had seen since leaving home in February, and was quite an event. The most interesting evening at Apsley

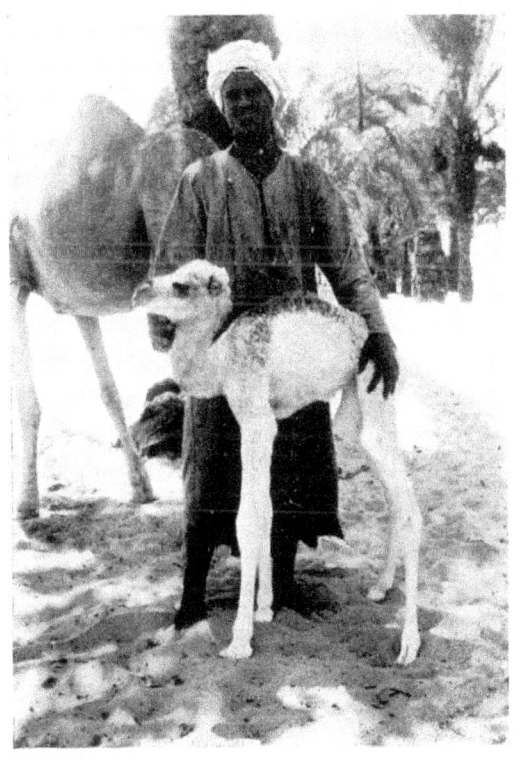

BABY CAMEL, THREE DAYS OLD

IN FRONT OF GAZA

House was one on which the Brigadier came to dine at Battalion H.Q. Mess, and after dinner unfolded to a few of us, under pledge of secrecy, the general plan of the campaign which was soon to open. It was a great conception, and with few alterations the plans were substantially those which were put into operation six weeks later. The Brigadier finished by telling us what also proved to be the case, that as long as the advance continued we would all be worked if necessary till we dropped, but at the end of operations would come a good rest and as much leave as possible.

A week or two previously I had unfortunately inherited from Robb Cree the job of Battalion Mess President, which at best is a very thankless task and one to which I was able to give very little attention. Rations were very good, and with the assistance of a weekly order from Fleurent in Cairo and many cases of bottles from Sandeman we were able to mess in modest luxury. " W " Company Officers' Mess in particular had acquired a great reputation for its culinary attainments, and an invitation to dinner from that quarter was not one to be lightly regarded. It was nothing to be faced with a menu of Hors d'oeuvres, Soup, Lobster Mayonaise, Joint, with fried potatoes and vegetables, a toothsome sweet, and an excellent savoury, all most daintily served, the whole being preceded, attended and followed by cocktails, champagne, port, coffee, liqueurs and a long "Perando." So even these days of preparation had their brighter moments. Moves, when they came, came suddenly, so after three weeks I went off one day with little warning to accompany Bruce Allan, the Staff Captain, to select a bivouac area for the Battalion near the sea, where it could rest for one night on the long trek to Sheikh Ajlin. The following night at dusk the Battalion moved down the Wadi Ghuzze, and I went on ahead with a small advance party to apportion the Company areas and have everything ready for the Battalion on its arrival. Battalion Headquarters were on the shore, and seemed delightfully fresh after the dust of Apsley House.

On the next night we were due to take over the coastal section of the line at Sheikh Ajlin from a Battalion of an English Brigade, and I went ahead to take over the Trench Stores, etc., from one of its Companies. The object of sending our Brigade to this sector was to make us familiar with the terrain on the sea side of Gaza, over which the British attack was later to be launched. Sheikh Ajlin itself consists of a white-domed mosque (rather the worse for occasional bombardment by the Turks) covering a tomb, with some garden enclosures and clumps of trees. The mosque stands on the cliff overlooking the beach, and our trenches were just in front of the gardens, with Battalion Headquarters a little to the rear. The Orderly-room, in which I spent most of the following days, and the Signal-office were fairly substantial, shrapnel-proof dug-outs, but the others were more or less unprotected. However, the Turkish artillery usually confined its attentions to the area behind the fire trenches and in front of Battalion Headquarters. The line of trenches was cut

IN FRONT OF GAZA

straight through the soft, deep sand, and hundreds of thousands of sandbags had been employed in the work. The Turkish artillery, which was always excellent, had made good shooting at the communication trenches, and parts of these were almost unrecognisable, except for heaps of broken sandbags.

Early one morning I went up with the F.O.O. to the Observation Post on the Mosque, and, with the aid of his telescope, had a wonderful view of the Turkish defences, which stretched in unbroken lines in front of the gardens of Gaza till they reached north to the sea at Sheikh Hasan. John Miller, the Intelligence Officer, with his scouts and his namesake from "X" Company, carried out one or two exciting patrols to Chocolate Ridge and Sugar Loaf, but our ten days at Sheikh Ajlin passed without any major incidents.

Along with other reinforcements which had arrived during the past two months were numerous additional batteries of Heavy and Field Artillery, and many of these were massed behind the coastal sector. These batteries, after preliminary registration, were quite dumb, and their presence formed part of the surprise packet awaiting the enemy. While we were at Sheikh Ajlin a dog was seen once or twice running along the shore toward the Turkish lines. It was thought that the animal might be the medium by which messages were carried from enemy agents behind our lines, but in spite of a vigilant watch, the dog was never bagged. For some months past our Intelligence Branch had frequently published information that certain enemy agents were known to be in our lines and had been seen in particular localities. As the description of these spies almost invariably ended up with the words "he is known to be a deadly shot," it left one rather disinclined to great enthusiasm for the detective business.

After our stay at Sheikh Ajlin the Brigade was ordered back to the Regent Park area to put the finishing touches to our training. This area was among the sand dunes just to the north of the Wadi Ghuzze, and came by its name owing to the fact that two palm trees and a clump of bushes had managed to sustain a precarious existence at that spot near some wells. The Battalion was relieved at night, but I preceded it in the afternoon with a small advance party—a job which seemed now to fall to me as a matter of course. Like many administrative jobs, it was usually a thankless one, the only satisfaction being in the knowledge that the companies on arrival had no delay in reaching their areas and that a hot meal was waiting in the dixies. During the next three weeks there was much detail work of an administrative character. Shrapnel helmets were issued for the first time; all surplus kits were dumped at Belah, and ammunition and equipment of all kinds were brought up to mobile scale.

As regards the assault on the Gaza defences, the plans were roughly as follows: The assault was to be carried out by the 54th Division (Major-General S. W. Hare) and the 156 Brigade of the 52nd Division, and the particular task assigned to our Brigade was the capture of Umbrella Hill and El Arish Redoubt, which were the two strongest

A SAND SLEDGE AT EL ARISH

IN FRONT OF GAZA

points in the opposing network of defences. They lay to the south-east of the systems to be attacked by the Battalions of the 54th Division, and their capture was the essential precedent to success.

General Leggett disposed the 156 Brigade as follows: The 7th Scottish Rifles was to assault and capture Umbrella Hill. To the 4th Royal Scots was assigned the capture and consolidation of the El Arish Redoubt system, and the 7th Royal Scots, being the strongest Battalion numerically, was at the outset held in reserve. The rôle of the 8th Scottish Rifles was a very strenuous one, but, being of many parts, did not unfortunately admit of the Battalion working as one unit. In addition to helping in the assault, we were also made responsible that R.E. material and ammunition would be immediately available on the spot, as consolidation and counter attack would succeed the capture of both positions. Three large dumps were formed immediately behind our front line, and of these Colonel Findlay was in charge of two, while Major Coulson was responsible for the other. "W" and "X" Companies were to supply the necessary carrying parties, while "Y" Company was detailed to take part in the assault with the 7th Scottish Rifles, and "Z" Company with the 4th Royal Scots.

The work of the three weeks at Regent's Park was all toward the perfection of these plans. The contents of the dumps were all arranged and divided into separate loads, each of which could conveniently be carried by one man, and all material was carefully scheduled and checked to ensure that no essential item was missing. Countless boxes of S.A.A. and Trench Mortar ammunition were carried up to the line and buried, and under the arrangements of John Nicholl, as Brigade Transport Officer, unending strings of camels carried their fanatis up to the forward water dumps. All these arrangements were carried through during darkness.

Robb Cree and M'Combie took their Companies away at intervals to practice the assault with the 7th Scottish Rifles and the 4th Royal Scots over dummy systems of trenches which had been sited to represent the real thing at Umbrella Hill and El Arish Redoubt. Sheaves of preliminary orders and administrative instructions poured in a daily stream into our Orderly-room, and Dulieu and I were fully employed in keeping our heads above water. Paint had to be procured for marking distinguishing signs on helmets, Battalion whistles had to be learned and practised by all ranks, and even a few phrases of Turkish became part of our vocabulary. Ollernshaw was busy with clothing and equipment, and Lewis guns were overhauled. New transport scales were compiled, and the weights of camel loads assessed. It was known that the assault would take place on or about 1st November, and during the week previous our heads positively buzzed with Orders and Instructions of all sorts. Artillery and machine-gun barrages, the names and routes to be taken by Tanks, the composition of the Nucleus and Administrative Portion, arrangements for the care of wounded, the burial of the dead, the disposal of prisoners, routes to be followed by the different

IN FRONT OF GAZA

units, forward bivouac arrangements, and the rôle to be played by the Navy were a few of the items to be discussed and digested.

Now at this point an unfortunate scandal occurred. Tanks were of two types, male and female, the male being provided with two three-pounders and the female with machine guns. On looking down the lists of Tanks detailed in Orders, it was noticed with regret that the Tank "Lady So and So" had left her proper place among the ladies and slipped in among the males. It required a further Divisional Order to reassure the anxious troops with the information that a mistake had occurred and that the bold "Lady So and So" had been replaced in her proper sphere. As one of the male Tanks was called the "Otazel," it was realised that the worst had been narrowly averted.

Considering the hectic life of these days, it was rather surprising and a little amusing to receive a telegram a few days before the battle instructing a few of us from the 156 Brigade to proceed to Divisional Headquarters to take part in a concert. However, Orders are Orders, so taking our batmen and our bivouacs, I rode down one afternoon with James Austin of the 7th Scottish Rifles to Sheikh Shabassi, where the Divisional Staff lived in an atmosphere of much splendour and great comfort. As all our songs had gone to the dump at Belah with our surplus kits, we had no music of any kind, and consequently approached the performance with some diffidence. This feeling was considerably increased when we found a magnificent stage erected in the open air, with such things as a good piano and electric footlights fixed up for the occasion. However, fortified by the hospitality of the Divisional Messes, the concert went off considerably better than we could have hoped. General Hill was very complimentary and hospitable, and we thoroughly enjoyed our day's rest.

One night at Regent's Park we encountered a very violent thunderstorm, accompanied by torrential rain and a gale of wind. When it began John Nicholl, who had come up from the Brigade Transport Mess to dine, accompanied me with all speed to my bivouac, where we crouched together on my bed under a waterproof. At first I attempted to keep a candle burning, but this was quite impossible owing to the gale, and our entire efforts were centred on keeping the bivouac from blowing away. The lightning was sufficiently bright to supply the illuminations. The stout canvas of the bivouac entirely failed in its efforts to keep out the rain, which positively splashed through on us. The crash and roll of the thunder mingled with the crack and boom of our guns, which were at the time carrying out a heavy bombardment, and the noise was deafening. The storm ultimately ceased as suddenly as it had begun, and we got busy with the work of repairs to our dwellings.

A day or two later came Brigade Operation Orders for the attack. These Orders are intensely interesting to those affected by them, but it is seldom that anything in the nature of sentiment is allowed to creep in among the paragraphs. However, the

IN FRONT OF GAZA

following was the last para. of the Orders as issued by General Leggett:

> "In this, the concluding para. of Operation Orders, the Brigadier-General Commanding wishes every officer, N.C.O. and man all possible good luck in the forthcoming action. He knows that nothing is going to stop the 156 Brigade; a brilliant success awaits it, and the honour shown to us in being selected to represent the 52nd Division is safe in its hands. The 156 Brigade has in the past taken many a position, killed many a Turk, captured many a prisoner, and never yet lost a single yard of trench. History will surely repeat itself in a few days from now in fullest measure, and, please God, Scotland will be proud of us and satisfied with our work."

It was anticipated that the assault would take place on the 1st November, but this could not be definitely fixed, as the attack on Gaza depended on the success of the operations at Beersheba, some thirty miles to the south-east. However, to be in readiness, the Brigade moved up to its forward area two nights before the expected date of the assault, and I went up with Miller in the afternoon to apportion areas to the Companies. The Battalion occupied some old disused and uncovered dug-outs on the reverse side of a sand dune situated a few hundred yards from the front line and near the entrance to the communication trenches. The Companies were well spread out, as the enemy artillery was likely to be active. On the morning of the 1st November we received a wire that Beersheba had been captured, and we realised that it was now our turn. On that forenoon Major-General Hare, under whose command the 156 Brigade was operating along with the 54th Division, came round to Battalion Headquarters and asked to be introduced to as many of our officers as could be gathered together. He had commanded the Scottish Rifle Brigade in the Falkirk days of 1914, and so felt quite among old friends. He spoke to us for a little while, and his courtesy and interest were much appreciated. His visit was of course not necessary, but it certainly showed us that we had come under the command of one who was something more than a mere General. From him we also learned that zero hour would fall that night. The Brigadier, with Franklin, the Brigade Major, called at Battalion Headquarters in the evening to wish us good luck. Then "Y" and "Z" Companies set out to join the assaulting Battalions, and after dark the other two Companies with Battalion Headquarters moved up to the respective dumps. As Assistant-Adjutant my job was to remain at the forward area with Ollernshaw and the administrative portion of Battalion Headquarters to deal with supplies and all details of administration.

Zero hour for the assault on Umbrella Hill was 10 p.m., and some time before that our artillery fire, which had steadily increased in volume for some days, reached the intensity of drum fire. Looking back toward our gun line, the darkness was gashed and torn by constant flashes, while the continuous bark of the field guns and the roar of the heavier pieces made conversation impossible. The air was alive with the whine of the shells overhead. The old Turk responded most vigor-

IN FRONT OF GAZA

ously, and the area behind our line became most unhealthy. Never in my life had I heard such a din, and reports and explosions were absolutely continuous. In the midst of this two Tanks waddled up past our position, leaving a trail of petrol smoke behind, which brought me suddenly back to the London streets.

Not long after 10 p.m. a wire reached me from Brigade reporting the successful capture of Umbrella Hill, and at 11 p.m. the 4th Royal Scots, with "Z" Company, launched their attack on the El Arish system. Complete success soon followed, and the work of the carrying Companies began. This was work which entailed the greatest possible determination and endurance. It was not carried out in the heat and excitement of an assault lasting a very short time, but entailed many weary trips backward and forward across the 600 yards of No Man's Land, undertaken more or less in cold blood and with the greatest fatigue. And all the time these six hundred yards were alive with shell bursts, and swept by enemy machine guns. The neighbourhood of the dumps was particularly unhealthy, but the carrying parties moved backwards and forwards with unfailing devotion. The Doctor was kept busy in his Aid Post, for the numbers of the parties were constantly thinning. Ollernshaw, with some men from our Headquarters, carried up dixies of hot tea to the front line, and had many unpleasant experiences on the way.

In the very early hours of the 2nd November I heard our sentry challenge someone, and I thought the reply came back in John Nicholl's voice. I shouted to him, but my voice could not carry above the general din, and I was too busy to leave my work. I was just able to notice in the gray light that it was someone leading two mules, with a wounded man on each. Later I found that I had been right, and that it was John Nicholl just returning from his hazardous share in the proceedings. Just after the 4th Royal Scots, with "Z" Company, had captured their position, he had started out across No Man's Land with some of his transport men and twenty-eight mules laden with ammunition and R.E. material. No Man's Land at the best of times is a most undesirable place, but to wander across it with twenty-eight mules in the midst of an intense artillery and machine-gun barrage is, to say the least of it, a highly dangerous occupation. However, by good leading and accompanied by a fair share of luck, the entire party got safely across, and every single box of ammunition was safely handed over. It was hardly to be expected that the same luck would hold out on the return journey, but this was completed with wonderfully few casualties to his men and the loss of only three mules. It was certainly a fine performance. Soon a slow stream of wounded began to filter past our little camp, and we did what we could to help them on their way back to the Advanced Dressing Stations.

At 4 a.m. on the 2nd the attack on the position stretching north-west to the sea was launched by the 54th Division on our left. One not unpleasant result to us was that a good proportion of the enemy artillery immediately switched its point of

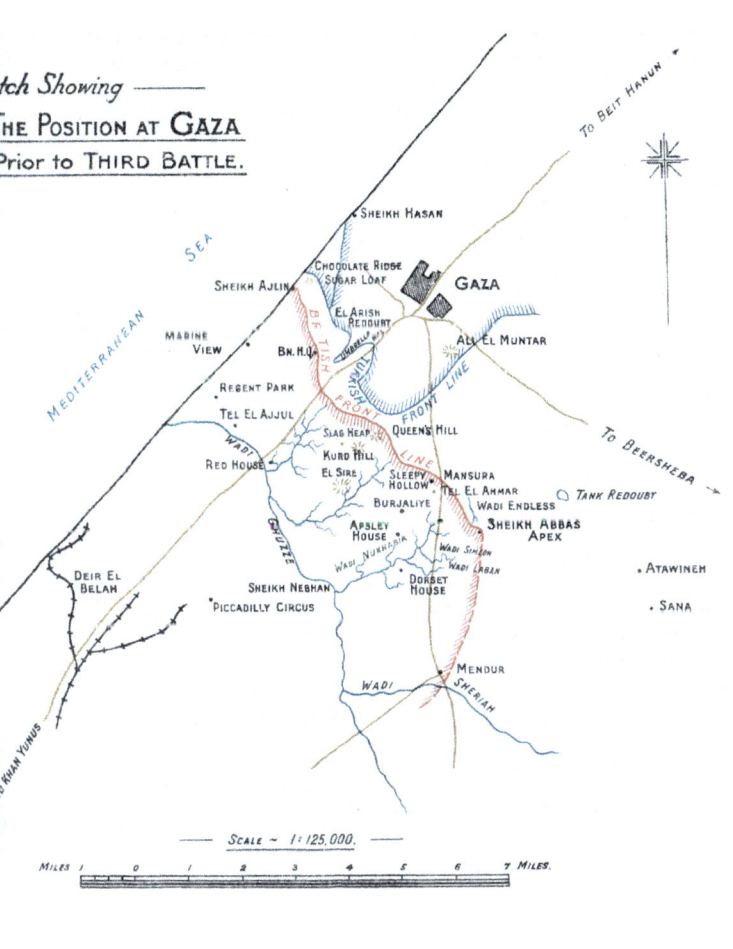

IN FRONT OF GAZA

concentration away from our sector. With the exception of one or two small localities, the attack by the 54th Division was successful, and consolidation of the captured line proceeded rapidly, though under very difficult and unhealthy conditions. The enemy trenches were a perfect shambles. Carswell had the job of establishing a Brigade Advance Signal Station in El Arish redoubt, and succeeded in keeping communication open with very few breaks. His Military Cross was well won. Some time in the evening of the 2nd one of the Tank commanders pushed his head into my shack and said he had lost his way. He represented one of the minor tragedies of battle, and was absolutely distraught from lack of sleep and food. He told me he had determined to do great deeds with his Tank, but through bad luck he had ended by doing two of the things he had determined at all hazards to avoid, for he had ditched his Tank beyond recovery, and lost a gun. He was quite desolate, but after some food and a drink he began to show signs of revival, and set out again to make arrangements for the recovery of his Tank. During the forenoon of the 2nd one of our Observation Balloons escaped from its moorings, and at a great height floated over the battlefield toward the north till it was lost to sight in the haze. These are only a few of the incidents which passed like a kaleidoscope, for so many events crowded in upon us during these days and nights and passed with such rapidity that only a general impression was left of the backwash of battle.

Meantime the enemy was in a very unhappy

position. The advance from the Beersheba flank was proceeding steadily, though hardly so rapidly as had been hoped, and while the threat from that side became daily more serious, he was pinned down to Gaza by our attack from the west. The employment and disposition of his reserves must have acutely exercised the mind of the Turkish Commander-in-Chief. The only logical conclusion seemed to be that he must retire from Gaza, but still he held on with surprising tenacity. The work at the dumps was now completed, and Battalion Headquarters, with "W" and "X" Companies, returned to the forward bivouac area. Full reports were now received, and all showed the complete success of the operations. The two assaulting Companies had done their full share, and the work of the carrying Companies was beyond all praise. The spirit of the men was wonderful. There had been sufficient pathos, tragedy and humour—the latter usually supplied by the wounded—to last the most exacting for a lifetime.

On the 3rd a message of thanks and congratulations was received from the Corps Commander. By the 5th the 7th Royal Scots had relieved the 4th Royal Scots at El Arish Redoubt, and the work of consolidation being well ahead in the captured positions, "Y" and "Z" Companies were able to rejoin the Battalion. During the night of the 6th/7th the Turks, with considerable skill, retired from their positions in and around Gaza. I was enjoying a good sleep that night, and when I wakened early in the morning there was a wonderful stillness and calm. I ran to the top of the sand

IN FRONT OF GAZA

dune in front of Headquarters, and looked away toward Gaza and the north. As far as the eye could reach every dune and hillock held small parties of our men looking in wonder toward the now silent city. Reorganisation of the Battalion began at once, and I was busy all day. In the evening I made a hasty visit to the enemy trenches at El Arish Redoubt. At many points they were destroyed beyond all recognition, and everywhere were strewn the flotsam and jetsam of battle. The wounded had all been evacuated, but the burial parties were busy collecting bodies for interment. An occasional rifle sticking up in the sand in No Man's Land showed the spot where some of our men still lay as derelicts after the storm. The chaos of these trenches was indescribable.

The following messages and Orders must close this very sketchy account of the Capture of Gaza and a few of the events which led to it :

(1) Copy of letter from Lieut.-Colonel A. M. Mitchell, Comdg. 1/4th Bn. The Royal Scots, to Lieut.-Colonel J. M. Findlay, Comdg. 1/8th Scottish Rifles, dated 5th November, 1917, and included here by permission :

"Dear Colonel Findlay,
I desire to express to you personally my thanks for the good work done by the Companies of your Battalion assisting my Battalion. The conduct and bearing of all ranks and the dash and determination with which the enemy works were carried, and the quiet steadiness of all ranks during consolidation and counter attacks, adds yet another fine record to the splendid record of British Infantry. I shall be glad if Captains Hannan and M'Combie will furnish me with the names

of N.C.O.'s and men whom they consider merit special recognition. I know there are several. I regret, as you will, the loss of so many good comrades, but I know none of us will forget the men who gave their lives so that success might be obtained. Might I ask you to convey to Officers, N.C.O.'s and Men who co-operated with the 4th Royal Scots on the 2nd and 3rd November my great appreciation of the work done by them.

"I am, yours sincerely,

(Sgd.) "MACLAINE MITCHELL, Lieut.-Colonel,
"Comdg. 1/4th Bn. The Royal Scots (Q.E.R.).

"5th November, 1917."

(2) Special Order by Lieut.-Colonel Romanes, D.S.O., Comdg. 1/7th Scottish Rifles, dated 5th November, 1917:

"Before 'W' and 'Y' Companies, 8th Scottish Rifles return to their own unit, the Commanding Officer wishes to put on record the infinite debt of gratitude that this unit owes to these two Companies. After the assault on Umbrella Hill, itself a task which 'Y' Company performed admirably, both these Companies, in a most gallant manner, went backward and forward through heavy enemy artillery barrage, whose intensity all ranks have appreciated, to carry the stores necessary for consolidation. For nearly thirty-six consecutive hours these Companies continued their work, to the nature of which their heavy casualty list is a melancholy tribute. Had such been previously lacking, the action of 1/2nd November, 1917, will be an unbreakable tie between the 7th and 8th Battalions.

(Sgd.) "HECTOR C. MACLEAN, Captain.
"For Comdg. Officer 1/7 Sco. Rifles.

"5th November, 1917."

(3) Message from Major-General S. W. Hare, Comdg. 54th Division, to Brigadier-General A. H. Leggett, Commdg. 156th Infantry Brigade,

dated 8th November, 1917, and published throughout the units of the Brigade:

> "Please convey to my old comrades and fellow countrymen of the Scottish Rifle Brigade my heartfelt thanks for the great part they have played in the late battle. The gallantry with which they captured their objectives and held them under several days of heavy shelling adds to the reputation they earned in the Gallipoli peninsula. Tell them that it has been a great pleasure to me to renew our old acquaintance, and to have them under me, especially now that the Brigade includes Battalions from Edinburgh and Leith, it is 'just like being at hame.'
>
> (Sgd.) "S. W. HARE,
> "Major-General.
>
> "8th November, 1917."

THROUGH THE LAND OF THE PHILISTINES

A STRATEGICAL DIGRESSION—WADI HESI—A RECONNAISSANCE BY MOUNTED INFANTRY—TO ASKALON AND MEJDEL—IN THE MARKET-PLACE OF ASHDOD—BURKAH—"HIDE AND SEEK" WITH THE BATTALION—A MUSICAL COMEDY AT EKRON—A FULL ACCOUNT OF THE HISTORY AND GLORIES OF RAMLEH.

To obtain a clearer perspective a very brief digression must here be made into the realms of higher strategy. The general idea of the Grand Attack was first to capture Beersheba, with its defensive systems, and then to send a strong force north by the Hebron road, and another in a north-westerly direction behind Gaza. Meantime, immediately on the capture of Beersheba a strong holding attack was to be launched against the defences of Gaza, so that the enemy would be pinned to his trenches, while some inducement would be offered to the Turkish Commander-in-Chief to throw in his Reserves on his right flank. After the break through at Beersheba, the pursuit was to be carried out entirely by the XXth Corps, which was operating on the right of our line, and it was not intended that the troops engaged at Gaza would

THE LAND OF THE PHILISTINES 63

take any part, except to follow on in the wake of the other Corps. To this end the camels allotted to us had been reduced as far as possible in numbers, and all surplus animals, motor-lorries and transport of every kind were lent to the XXth Corps. What actually occurred, however, was that the attack on our right by the XXth Corps was held up and delayed, while the Turk by his skilful retiral from Gaza had succeeded in extricating his right flank, and was now preparing to retreat along the coastal route.

General Allenby therefore decided to change the original plan, and to carry out a vigorous pursuit with the available troops and reduced transport of the XXIst Corps, then in the Gaza sector. The troops of this Corps consisted of the 52nd, 54th and 75th Divisions. The 75th Division was employed holding the line east of Gaza—opposite Tank and Ataweeneh Redoubt Systems—and could not move until the situation in that sector was finally cleared up.

The 54th Division and the 156 Brigade were not immediately available, being now in the captured positions and being to a certain extent disorganised after their five days' continuous fighting. As for the remainder of the 52nd Division, the 155 Brigade was holding the original line from which our attack had been launched, while the rôle of the 157 Brigade during the battle had been that of general reserve. And so, when pursuit became possible, the only troops concentrated and available for the purpose were the 157 Brigade, which was lying at Marine View, and one Squadron of Corps

Cavalry. The Commander-in-Chief therefore ordered General Hill, with the 52nd Division, to begin the pursuit of the retreating enemy at 8 a.m. on the 7th November. The 157 Brigade immediately set off, and was followed at about noon by the 155 Brigade. For the 156 Brigade the day of the 7th November was particularly crowded, and no one had a moment's rest.

Our own Battalion had been continuously engaged for five days and five nights without respite, and everyone had reached a stage bordering on complete exhaustion. From noon on the 6th the enemy kept up a continuous and heavy bombardment on the captured positions. Later we learned that one of his objects was to fire off all his gun ammunition, so that on his retiral none might be left to fall into our hands. But even now there was little chance for rest. Owing to the considerable number of casualties, complete reorganisation of the Companies was essential, and, in addition, the evacuation of wounded was completed, the dead were buried, and Casualty Returns compiled and checked. Ammunition was drawn and issued, rifles and Lewis guns cleaned, and all equipment finally brought up to mobile scale. There was very little sleep for anyone on the night of 7/8th November.

General Leggett had allowed himself until 8 a.m. on the 8th to get under weigh with the Brigade, but before daylight broke on that day our Battalion camels—78 in number—with the ammunition and Lewis gun limbers, had arrived from the Transport lines, and loading was in full swing. By 5 a.m. the

CATERPILLARS DRAGGING HEAVY GUNS ALONG THE SHORE BETWEEN GAZA AND ASKALON, 8TH NOV. 1917

(In the distance ships of the Royal Navy are shelling the retreating enemy)

THE LAND OF THE PHILISTINES 65

Battalion, after taking up its allotted place in the Brigade Column, had marched off, and the camel convoy and limbers moved down to take their place with the Transport. We crossed over in a direct line to the shore, and struck the beach just to the south of Sheikh Ajlin. It was a lovely morning, and spirits were high at the thought of leaving Gaza behind and seeing new country. I rode with John Nicholl, and away ahead, almost as far as the eye could see, stretched the long column of troops and transport. There were Batteries of Field Artillery, with ten-horse gun teams and heavy guns drawn by caterpillars, ploughing through the deep sand.

We soon passed the Turkish wire, which stretched across the shore right into the water, and came abreast of Sheikh Hasan. We would have made a splendid target for enemy airmen, but fortunately our Flying Corps had by now gained a complete mastery, and we were absolutely unmolested. The sand was soft and deep, which made the going very heavy, and the men were carrying double rations and an increased supply of ammunition. Farther north the Navy was busy, and we could see the flashes of the ships' guns as they harried the enemy in their retreat. John Nicholl had managed to bring along a little assortment of mess stores, and about 10 a.m., aided by a jack-knife and our fingers, we made fine play with a tin of peaches. Lying derelict on the beach we found our old friend the Tank "Otazel," with its port ped-rail badly twisted. To all appearance a shell must have exploded directly underneath it.

Just after noon we came up on Divisional Headquarters, and found the Brigade halted close by the shore. Though we could see ahead the white puffs of shrapnel and the black bursts of H.E., and knew that the other Brigades of the Division were in touch with the retreating enemy, the situation in front was apparently not sufficiently clear, so while we waited for further orders, we improved the occasion by securing some lunch and a rest. I was hailed over to where Humble and the "W" Company officers were sitting, and helped to dispose of an excellent meal, which seemed suddenly to arrive from nowhere. A cheering sight was an enemy plane which was shot down by one of our airmen and crashed a few miles inland. Then came Orders, and we were soon on the move again. After about three miles the pace became much slower, and we had many long checks. The other two Brigades were busy ahead. There were many dark objects lying on the beach, and the little breeze carried toward us the sound of the guns and the stench of dead horses. The sappers were already busy boring their wells in the sand, and we were stopped for a long while at the Wadi Hesi, for the Turk was shelling the crossing. We knew that the Battalion was across the wadi and was a mile or two inland, but otherwise our knowledge of its position was hazy.

When the shelling at the wadi slackened it had begun to get dark, a process which in Palestine comprises only a very brief interlude before night closes down. To find a Battalion Headquarters in the dark and in unknown country is no easy job,

THE LAND OF THE PHILISTINES 67

so we decided to push on, and took the camels across the wadi in batches of tens, at 200-yard distances. The wadi at its mouth must be nearly half a mile broad, so we crossed at a wide angle, making for a point on the other side about a mile inland. There seems to be some kindly Providence which guides a camel convoy to its haven, for we soon found Battalion Headquarters, which was situated in the open among patches of sandy scrub. Two of the Companies were already in position on some high ground which had been captured earlier in the day by the 157 Brigade, and a little later the Colonel joined us on his return from a reconnaissance of the line.

While we were having dinner we heard the sentry challenge, and a Yeomanry officer was brought along to where we were sitting. A troop of Yeomanry which had been operating in the open country well ahead of the Infantry had failed to report, and this officer was anxious to set out at once to look for them. It seemed a hopeless quest in the darkness, but he was determined not to lose a minute in starting his search, and without waiting for any food, pushed on to where he would pass through the outpost line into the blue beyond. And so he disappeared into the night, and we heard no more news of the lost troop. Later we often wondered what had been its fate.

Our job with the Convoy in these days hinged immediately on the fighting disposition of the Battalion, and the general situation was usually possible of comprehension, but the dispositions on this night at the Wadi Hesi seemed as difficult to penetrate as the night itself. We appeared to know nothing of the enemy's movements and very little of our other two Brigades or the position on our flanks. It is an uncomfortable feeling. However, the night passed quietly, and dawn ushered in a day, the loveliness of which made warfare seem a double crime. We heard the first rumours of the stiff fighting which the 157 Brigade had experienced near Herbieh, some little way inland, and we waited momentarily expecting orders to move.

Many things happened which we only learned at a later date, and it was often difficult to appreciate at the moment the real meaning of incidents as they occurred, for they were all woven into the fabric of larger operations. It appeared that during the evening of the 8th and up to 3 a.m. on the 9th the Turk had held tenaciously to the heights above Wadi Hesi, which served to cover the inland road from Gaza along which his garrisons from Tank and Ataweeneh Redoubts were endeavouring to escape. The 155 and 157 Brigades attacked these heights on a line roughly parallel to the coast. Our Brigade was in reserve, one of the Battalions being used to close the gap between the left of the 155 Brigade and the shore. Before final success was achieved the 157 Brigade repeatedly took and lost these heights, and though it was a quiet night for the 156 Brigade, it was a night of desperate fighting for the others.

The Battalion Scouts, who were always prepared at a moment's notice to exploit the resources of any neighbourhood, were not long in discovering an excellent orange grove, and though the fruit

BRINGING IN THE WOUNDED ON CACOLETS, WADI-HESI.

THE LAND OF THE PHILISTINES 69

was still green on the skin, the oranges were large, juicy and sweet. About midday we received orders to join the other Battalions near Brigade Headquarters on the beach, and in the afternoon we moved down across the sand dunes to the shore. A strong breeze sprang up from the west, and refused to let us forget the dead horses which were lying here and there near the water's edge. It is not a fragrant memory. The breeze increased in violence, and as it carried with it clouds of fine sand, the picnic life was not too pleasant. I managed, however, to get my bivouac erected in the lee of a sand dune, and so was able to secure for Dulieu and myself some little protection.

As the process of erection was nearing completion I saw Captain T. M'Clelland, the Assistant Brigade-Major, riding past toward Brigade Headquarters with a quaint-looking mounted party of six or eight, some of whom were riding without even saddles. It was some time later that I heard of the doings of this assorted troop of mounted Infantry and the very useful job it had carried through. It seemed that the situation in the neighbourhood of Askalon was somewhat obscure on that morning, and the higher command was anxious to find out the exact position. There was no Cavalry available at the moment for a reconnaissance, so the Brigadier sent off M'Clelland with a scratch mounted troop composed of signallers and grooms from Brigade Headquarters to do the job. The eight-mile ride to Askalon was certainly adventurous, but, with the exception of riding down a sniper *en route* who was armed with a very fine automatic rifle, it passed without much incident. Askalon was found to be free of any enemy, so M'Clelland decided to push on four miles northeast to Mejdel to see what he could find there. On reaching the village he pushed boldly up the little street, leaving two men as a rearguard. There seemed to be few people about, but he noticed two armed Turkish soldiers disappearing hurriedly through a gateway. He was not sure whether they had run with the object of rousing a garrison, but taking the risk, he immediately followed. Inside he found fortunately that there was no garrison, but a large store of ammunition and other material, which the enemy had apparently been unable to move. He was engaged in wondering what to do with his capture when a squadron of Australian Cavalry, which had just arrived, rode into the village. Now Australians have acquired the habit of being the earliest arrivals on all such occasions, and the officer in command very apparently did not relish the fact that at Mejdel they could only take second place, and that to a scratch troop of Infantry. The climax of the situation was reached when M'Clelland formally handed over the captured dump to the Australians and requested and obtained a receipt from the Officer in Command, and this receipt was safely in his pocket when I saw him and his party pass by about 7 p.m. on their return to report to Brigade Headquarters.

As the night wore on the breeze increased, and we messed in my shack, as it happened to be the roomiest. It was considered a very comfortable bivouac for one, but on this occasion the party

THE LAND OF THE PHILISTINES

inside consisted of Colonel Findlay, Major Coulson, Dulieu, Innes, Miller, John Nicholl, the Doctor and myself. There was some idea that we might be left in our present location for a day or two, but the rumour turned out to be one bred of excessive optimism, and at 11 p.m., when Dulieu and I were asleep, an Orderly pushed his way into the shack with orders from Brigade. These entailed a move at 7 a.m. next morning, and as orders had to be sent out at once to the Companies and all arrangements set on foot, our night was rather disturbed.

The Battalion moved off in the early morning of the 10th, and the camel convoy waited to bring on the rations, which were expected to arrive with a big divisional convoy in the forenoon. The long convoy brought with it two days' rations for our Battalion, and the transfer of these to our own camels necessitated considerable alteration of the loads. To enable us to carry the essentials a number of things had to be jettisoned, and among these was a drum of cresol, which I later found had been one of the Doctor's most cherished possessions. The fate of a cresol drum to an M.O. is almost a personal affair, and for some time after its loss I was conscious of a slight coldness from medical quarters. In the early afternoon the convoy was again on the road, and we plodded through deep sand toward the dark promontory on which are the remains of Askalon. About 5 p.m. we had reached the headland and turned eastward from the shore. The sandy road from the beach was steep, and John Nicholl had to put double teams in the limbers.

On the outskirts of Askalon are the usual garden enclosures, with cactus hedges and a few modern houses. The Navy had made good practice with the latter, and as residences they now looked somewhat draughty and unsafe. We crossed the Turkish trenches which had guarded the position, and followed along the broad track left in the sand by the Infantry. At this point dusk closed in, and we looked forward to the usual hunt in the dark to find the Battalion. Fortunately, however, M'Alpin, the Brigade Camel Officer, met us and agreed to act as guide. A couple of miles farther on we came out on to more open country and harder ground, and the twinkling lights of candles and cook-fires showed us where the Brigade was lying. It was pitch dark when we eventually found our way to Battalion Headquarters beside the village of Mejdel. On arrival we learned that, owing to the great difficulties of supply so far from railhead, General Leggett had put the Brigade on half-rations. The water difficulties were also acute, and at Mejdel many horses belonging to the Australians, New Zealanders and Yeomanry, who had crossed over from the Beersheba flank, were watered for the first time in forty-eight hours.

We spent the night sleeping under the trees, and prepared for an early start in the morning. The Colonel succeeded in discovering a large granary, which proved a most useful find. At 9 a.m. on the 11th the Brigade column moved from Mejdel *en route* for Esdud (Ashdod). The convoy followed immediately behind, and we passed through a perfect maze of gardens and enclosures before reaching

THE LAND OF THE PHILISTINES 73

open country. A slight Khamseen was blowing, but its discomfort was considerably lessened by the plentiful supply of oranges, which were usefully employed to slake our thirst. At one point the country seemed to become one vast field of thistles, which were not pleasant for the barefooted camelmen.

At 3 p.m. we reached some rising ground just to the south of Esdud, where the Staff of the 157 Brigade was directing an engagement against the Turkish rearguards. After halting for about an hour, we moved up into the village, where the Battalion was bivouacked among the gardens at one side of the market-place. Battalion Headquarters was in a very dusty spot beside the old water-wheel. Shells were landing around the outskirts of the village, and the enemy showed considerable activity. At this point it became clear that the Turks had been able to reduce the disorganisation of retreat to some semblance of order, and it seemed certain that they would make a determined stand on the rising ground near Burkah, about two and a half miles distant. This determination was due to the fact that the Burkah line was one of the last suitable positions left to the enemy at which he could defend the Jaffa-Jerusalem railway.

In the early morning of the 12th the Colonel was called to Brigade Headquarters to discuss the projected attack on the enemy position. At 11 a.m. the Battalion fell in, in fighting kit, and marched out of the village to take its part with the Brigade in driving the enemy from the Burkah position. I was to be prepared to follow with the convoy at shortest notice, but to await further orders. The Artillery fire increased, and a little later the Infantry became heavily engaged. As the day wore on at Esdud Ollernshaw drew two days' rations and a further water supply, but still no orders reached us from the Battalion. As dusk was approaching I got rather anxious, and sent a runner to Brigade Headquarters to find out if the Battalion required ammunition, rations or water. As a result of those enquiries, John Nicholl and Ollernshaw set out in the dark with sufficient camels to carry the necessary rations, etc. Our idea of the exact location of the Battalion was rather indefinite, but after some experiences they succeeded in finding Headquarters, and handed over the supplies. They did not get back to Esdud till 5 a.m. on the 13th, but were able to bring with them a sketchy account of the battle.

The Brigade had been called upon to advance over an open plain devoid of any cover with the object of capturing a prepared line of trenches held by several thousand Turks with about fifty Machine Guns and supported by Artillery. After an attack in the heat of the day, with practically no water, the objective was finally taken at midnight. In the course of the action the 4th Royal Scots, on the right of the Brigade line, met with fierce fighting, and sustained very heavy casualties. Although the engagement at Burkah was in every respect a full-dress battle, carrying with it results of first-class importance, it is rather curious to note that the reference to this day in General Allenby's

THE LAND OF THE PHILISTINES

Official Despatch is "The 12th was spent in preparation for the attack...." The attack mentioned apparently refers to the subsequent attack on the 13th November against the Katrah-Mughar line, and no mention whatever is made of the Battle of Burkah.

Shortly after 8 a.m. on the 13th I received a chit from Dulieu with orders to bring on the convoy and join the Battalion that night at Mughar, some eight miles farther north. I learned later that at the time I received this message Mughar itself was still in the hands of the retreating enemy, but its capture was expected before nightfall. The runner who brought the message also told me that Robb Cree was wounded, and had been evacuated to a Field Ambulance. I was sorry I could not take the time necessary to try to find him. The position on the morning of the 13th was made clear in the first paragraph of Operation Orders, which reached the Battalion in the small hours of that morning. The paragraph was as follows:

> "The Divisional Commander wishes all ranks to be informed that to-day, 13th inst., will be the decisive day of the war as far as Turkey is concerned, and that, hardly as everyone has been tried, we have got to make a superhuman effort to-day. The Commander-in-Chief intends to seize the Jaffa-Jerusalem Railway..."

Shortly after 10 a.m. the convoy was on the move, and we soon left behind us the dusty lanes and flat-roofed mud huts of Esdud. A rolling country opened out in front, and our first objective was the point in the wadi at Burkah, which had been the Headquarters of the Battalion on the previous night. Here we picked up some details which had been left behind by the Battalion, and pushed on across the battlefield. Here and there khaki-clad figures showed above the grass, and the burial parties were busy. The Turkish trenches made a formidable line, but had received rough handling from our Artillery, and broken machine-guns, rifles and all kinds of debris lay scattered around. At intervals we passed little groups of dead horses. These had been employed in Turkish gun-teams, and made a pathetic sight, as many seemed to have given up the fight owing to starvation, for their ribs almost cut through their flanks. On the way we fell in with Padre Semple, and as he had lived for some years in Palestine, he proved a useful guide.

Operations now took the form of a grand sweep forward on a two-divisional front (52nd and 75th Divisions), with a cavalry screen ahead In spite of all that claimed our immediate attention and the battle which we could see rolling on ahead of us, the picture of the country round was one of great loveliness. The day was bright and clear, and the Judean hills with their steep defiles, rocky spurs and deep re-entrants stood out in all the grandeur of dancing sunlight and deepest shade. The Padre pointed out the site of ancient Gath nestling at the foot of the hills to the east.

Then the battle seemed to slow down, and on the orders of one of the Divisional Staff we halted for a long time just behind a battery of our field guns which were in action. We had very little idea of

JOHN MILLER   E. R. B.
AT THE ORANGE GROVE NEAR WADI HESI

THE LAND OF THE PHILISTINES 77

the position of the Battalion, but as we were following the signal cable which led to the 156 Brigade Headquarters we had little anxiety. Dusk was just closing in when we found out the position of Brigade Headquarters, and John Nicholl rode over to find out the whereabouts of the Battalion. When he got back he could only report that the Battalion had temporarily passed under the orders of the G.O.C. 157 Brigade, which was in touch with the retreating enemy on our left and endeavouring to prevent him halting on the Mughar-Katrah line. Our own Brigade Staff knew nothing of the location of our own Battalion. This was rather disheartening.

It was now quite dark, and we were still some three-and-a-half miles from Mughar, but from the direction which the fighting had taken during the day, we felt quite sure that the Battalion had not reached Mughar, and we must look for it elsewhere. So John Nicholl, who, though apt to spurn the assistance of maps or compass, is blessed with an extraordinary faculty for finding things in the dark, set out on his wise old horse over a difficult and quite unknown country to run the Battalion to earth. He was away for nearly an hour, and I was just considering the sending out of another search party when I heard his hail come out of the darkness. How he had found the Battalion I never quite knew, but he was able to report its exact position, and he led us with the assurance of a blood-hound over rough country and across wadis until we found the Battalion bivouacked alongside the 7th Scottish Rifles in some gardens on the outskirts of the village of Beshshit. The Battalion seemed as surprised and relieved to see us as we were to find them, and the two-days' rations which we carried made us doubly welcome.

Eventually we learned of the very stiff action of the 155 Brigade on that day. This Brigade had been hotly engaged since morning in the vicinity of Katrah, and it was not until midnight that the firing died down. Katrah was entered at dawn on the 14th. During the course of the fighting the 155 Brigade, in spite of repeated efforts, was held up at one point until Brigadier-General Pollok M'Call, who was in command, went forward with rifle and bayonet in hand and personally led the attack, which resulted in complete success. General Allenby's Official Despatch refers to this engagement as follows:

> "This Katrah-El-Mughar line forms a very strong position, and it was here that the enemy made his most determined resistance against the turning movement directed against his right flank. The capture of this position by the 52nd (Lowland) Division, assisted by a most dashing charge of mounted troops, who galloped across the plain under heavy fire and turned the enemy's position from the north, was a fine feat of arms. Some 1100 prisoners, 3 guns, and many machine-guns were taken here."

In the evenings when the Convoy reached the Battalion there usually came an opportunity for a good square meal of bully beef stew or "Maconnachie," helped on its way by the excellent cocoa ration. Then followed wonderful nights when we slept with the starry heavens for our roof.

Orders for the 14th showed that we were to operate with the 157 Brigade, and were to carry on the pursuit, passing through the line captured by the 155 Brigade and striking out toward Mansurah.

Early that morning the Battalion moved out in support of the 5th A. & S.H., and our convoy followed immediately behind. Beshshit is quite a large native village, with quaint little mud huts shaped like small haystacks, crazy water-wheels, a girdle of cactus and palm trees, and illimitable dust. When we reached Katrah (Cedron), which was about a mile-and-a-half distant, we stopped to water the horses at an excellent well, where the R.E.'s had been busy. There had been some good houses in Katrah, but artillery fire had left them many scars, and the road which passed over the hill through the middle of the village was pitted with deep shell holes. For miles around the country was of a rolling character, but here and there little hills had pushed their heads up above the general level, and on each clustered a village, which showed an occasional red roof and clumps of palm trees. It was all very picturesque.

As we were climbing up the hill into Katrah a loud explosion, followed by clouds of smoke, a few miles east told that an important strategical success had been achieved and that a stretch of the Jaffa-Jerusalem line had been destroyed. This feat was carried out by Major Rolling, of the 412th Field Company R.E. (attached to 156 Brigade). He was accompanied only by two of his Officers, and to attain his object had ridden right out into the blue, far in advance of any of our troops. Earlier in the morning a train was seen steaming north from Junction Station. This was the last enemy train to get through, and it was learned afterwards that one of its passengers was Kress Von Kressenstein, the German General who commanded one of the Turkish Army Corps.

I was glad to spend a few minutes with Steven Bilsland at Katrah, but we could not delay long, so after the horses had been watered, we pushed on to Shahmeh, in which neighbourhood we hoped to find the Battalion. We found Humble's Company, which had just been released from its three days' job as escort to the guns, and joined them in a meal near the Wadi Merubbah. In the afternoon we found that the expected battle had been something in the nature of a bloodless victory, and we were able to push out into the open, where we found the Battalion at about 1 p.m. One important piece of work which fell to the credit of our Battalion Scouts was to get into touch with the 75th Division, which was operating on our right. We had to wait in the open for some little time for orders, and we watched the practice of a Turkish mountain gun shelling some camels which were moving across the plain about a quarter of a mile away. The camel is an excellent animal under fire, and treats all forms of warfare with complete contempt. The only drawback is that he has a deep-seated objection to hurrying at any time. At night we bivouacked by the edge of a little wadi near by, the companies being spread out fan shape, with the

BATTALION HEADQUARTERS BESIDE THE WELL AT ESDUD (ASHDOD)

THE LAND OF THE PHILISTINES

centre facing north-west. Junction Station, where the Jaffa-Jerusalem line meets the southern branch to Beersheba, was now in our hands, and the enemy seemed for the moment to have vanished. Owing to the speed of our pursuit, we were now more than thirty-five miles in advance of our railhead, and the question of supplies and transport must have caused the gravest anxiety to the Higher Command.

The 15th November was in the nature of an interlude, when orders and counter orders followed in bewildering succession. A number of N.C.O.'s and men were presented by the Divisional Commander with decorations won at Gaza, and to the genuine grief of all ranks, a telegram was received reporting that Robb Cree had died in hospital at Belah from his wounds received at Burkah. It is a great dispensation of providence that the conditions of warfare set apart very little time for grieving over personal losses, but everyone felt that in Robb Cree we had lost a very gallant comrade. So mixed are the tragedies and comedies of campaigning life that the next message received ran as follows:

" In view of casualties do you still require number of New Year cards ordered."

It would be safe to say that the subject of New Year cards had not entered the brain of a single officer or man of the Battalion from the days at Regent's Park before Gaza, when the original order for the cards was given, until that moment. It is wonderful to have a Staff who think of everything.

During the day the Battalion moved over to Akir (Ekron), which was about a mile away to the north-west. The Companies took up an outpost line on the north-west fringe of the village, and Battalion Headquarters took possession of the village school.

On 15th November the following message was published throughout all units of the 156 Brigade:

> The Commander-in-Chief personally visited 156 Brigade Headquarters this afternoon, and desired the Brigadier General Commanding to convey to all ranks of the Brigade his high appreciation of the good and gallant services of every man in the Brigade, and his warmest congratulations on the great and glorious results they have achieved.
>
> The Brigadier General Commanding in publishing the Commander-in-Chief's message would like to add one of his own, viz.: " I thank you one and all from the bottom of my heart. Greater sacrifice, greater endurance, greater fighting power have never been shewn by any troops in the history of our Empire than you Officers and Men of the 156 Brigade have shewn since the night of the 1/2 Nov. You have answered to every call, and victory has crowned your every effort. WELL DONE. The old folks at home will indeed be pleased and proud of you also, but there is no one, I think, who can be quite as pleased and proud as your Brigadier is of you all to-day.
>
> (Signed) T. A. FRANKLIN, Captain,
> Brigade Major, 156 Infantry Brigade.

15/11/17.

Ekron in ancient days was one of five chief cities of the Philistines, but is now a Jewish colony, founded by Rothschild in 1884. There are a

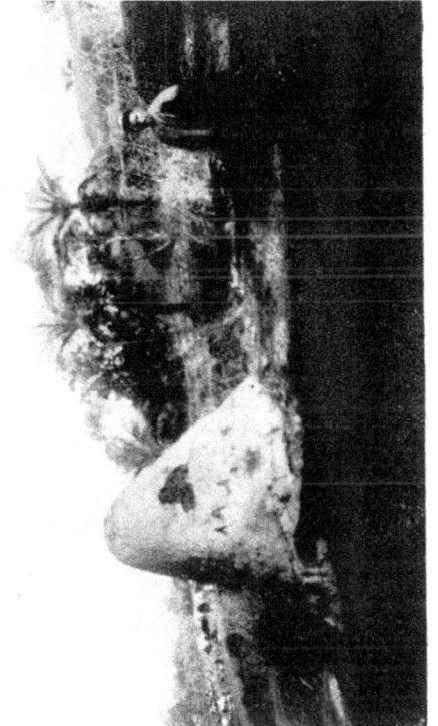

A NATIVE HOUSE AT BESHSHIT

THE LAND OF THE PHILISTINES 83

number of good substantial wooden houses, and it boasts an unusual attraction in public baths, which, although of a very primitive nature, provided a good wash for the entire Battalion. On the first night Battalion Headquarters Mess dined in the schoolmaster's house in considerable state, but as the entertainment consisted more or less of granting an audience to the principal men of the village and providing them with drinks from our slender stock, we decided that we would find more relaxation and economy by dining by ourselves in the schoolhouse. At that meal I tasted for the first time raisin jam, which, it seemed to me, would make an excellent substitute for tooth paste.

The accommodation in the schoolhouse was by no means princely, and on the first night I shared a room with the Colonel, Dick Coulson and Dulieu. The Colonel and Dick Coulson had beds of sorts, while Dulieu and I slept on our valises on the floor. Dick Coulson's bed was of a peculiarly musical type, for at his every breath it emitted a jangling of the springs, which became very monotonous. Some people seem to be possessed of bodies which appear to offer few attractions to the little things which creep and jump about in such happy hunting grounds as the schoolhouse at Ekron, but poor Dulieu was unfortunately not one of these. He seemed to spend the greater part of the night in an exhaustive hunt for little strangers in his valise. He told me that the quarry had spent the night jumping off his bed on to the floor, and had wakened him up with the noise of their hobnail boots. We spent the 16th and 17th in the same quarters, and were able to introduce some additional comforts.

While at Ekron we had one most humorous experience. It was necessary to collect from the inhabitants all implements of war of which they might be possessed, and the collection was made the occasion for a thoroughly imposing and, incidentally, comic ceremony. Opposite the entrance to the school was an open space, and one morning the Colonel read a proclamation to the people of the village to the effect that all arms and warlike material must be delivered up forthwith.

The Mayor had assembled the entire population along two sides of a square. Another side was occupied by the school children, dressed in white and marshalled by their teachers, while along the remaining side was drawn up one of our Companies, just to give the ceremony a thoroughly formal and military appearance. In the middle were the Colonel, Major Coulson, Dulieu, the Mayor and an interpreter. The Colonel in measured tones read out the proclamation, each sentence being translated after him by the interpreter, while the Guard of Honour, just to help on the general effect, presented arms at short intervals.

Having no specific part in the play, I made my way round the outskirts of the crowd, and going into an empty house, brought out a chair, on which I stood to take some photographs. The crowd was very silent and impressed, and when the Colonel finished his reading, the school children

LIEUT.-COL. J. M. FINDLAY READING THE PROCLAMATION AT EKRON

THE LAND OF THE PHILISTINES 85

advanced toward him singing and dancing. It was a great show, and if the Mayor had only been possessed of a lovely daughter to take the part of principal girl, instead of an aggressively plain and buxom spouse, we could have transferred the whole scene to a London theatre and played during a record run to crowded houses.

The proclamation, however, had the desired effect, for during the succeeding hour there was a constant stream of villagers making their way to the verandah at Battalion Headquarters carrying the most weird assortment of weapons and firearms. There were ancient Arab sabres with ivory handles, smaller swords and daggers, long Arab blunderbusses, rough leather belts filled with ancient and villainous blunt-nosed cartridges, spare parts of machine guns, excellent automatic revolvers, long pistols with carved handles and hammer action, modern shot guns, a gunsmith's appliances for the manufacture of cartridges, thousands of rounds of ammunition, and countless other weapons of all dates from barbaric times to the present day. The royal armoury at Madrid could hardly provide a more varied display.

During the two days we were at Ekron the cavalry had been busy, and we heard that the Australians had occupied Jaffa. Orders to move reached us on the 17th, and we looked forward to a rest and refit at Ramleh. Early on the morning of the 18th the Colonel set out with the Brigadier on a long reconnaissance. The Battalion, with the Convoy, marched out from Ekron at 9 a.m., and we made our way across country to a point where we would strike the Jaffa-Jerusalem road, just to the east of Ramleh. It was a lovely day, and the distant view of the town, with its sycamores, palm trees and lofty tower, was very imposing. As is the case with many eastern towns, the distant impression of grandeur failed entirely to stand the test of closer inspection. By 2 p.m. we had struck the main road—the first metalled road I had seen since crossing the Suez Canal—and found our way to the open ground east of the town, where the Brigade was concentrated.

With a determination to lose no chance of seeing anything of interest, John Nicholl and I obtained leave to visit the town in the afternoon. We saw a number of wrecked aeroplanes which the Turks had left behind, but the town itself was a grave disappointment. Its houses were poor, broken-down hovels, and filth and evil smells its highest distinction. An unpleasant black dust lay inches deep on the roads, and the bazaars were squalid and filled with the dirtiest assortment of loafers. To the west of the town there is a large and modern Franciscan Convent, which occupies the traditional site of the house of Joseph of Arimathea. In 1799 Napoleon occupied one of the rooms in the Convent, and to-day the pennant of the Headquarters of a Cavalry Division fluttered over the gateway. Sight-seeing at Ramleh need not be a lengthy business, and we soon made our way back to the Battalion, looking forward to a few days of rest.

In Sir Edmund Allenby's Official Despatch the task accomplished up to date by the troops of the XXIst Corps is summed up as follows:

> The Troops after their heavy fighting at Gaza had advanced in nine days a distance of about 40 miles, with two severe engagements and continual advanced guard fighting. The 52nd (Lowland) Division had covered 69 miles in this period.

THE SONG OF THE CAMEL CONVOY

We must follow, we must follow, the Battalion's on the way:
  Are the camels ready barracked, for it's past the break o' day?
Rouse the lagging Gippy drivers, get the loads adjusted fast,
  The Infantry is on the trek, the Guns are moving past.

We must follow with the convoy till the job is fully done,
  Over sand-dune, scrub and wadi, 'neath a blazing noon-day sun;
Over rock and stone and boulder, up the friendless pathless hill,
  When the sweat runs cold and chilly 'neath the rain-drenched khaki drill:
We must follow through the darkness of a night that's black and blind;
  We must search for dregs of humour where there's not a drop to find.

Though we're hungry, wet and weary, there is credit in the trip
  For the man who keeps on going and the loads that do not slip;
Till we've reached the lost battalion and the convoy's work is past,
  When the Rations and the Water are delivered safe at last.

AMONG THE HILLS

THE JOYS OF NIGHT MARCHING—SOME PECULIARITIES OF ROMAN ROADS—BEIT LIKIA—THE SPIRIT OF THE MEN—WANDERINGS AMONG THE HILLTOPS—TO KUBEIBEH (EMMAUS) AND NEBY SAMWIL—EVENTFUL DAYS—BULLY BEEF AND BISCUITS—A CALM BETWEEN TWO STORMS—BEIT SIRA—BACK TO THE PLAINS.

On our return to the Camp, and while we were still at some distance from it, we noticed signs of bustle and activity which seemed to portend a sudden move. We had certainly expected a day or two to rest and refit, but military life being full of the unexpected, such things as sudden moves become part of ordinary routine. When we reached Battalion Headquarters we found we were to take the road again at 7 p.m., and that our immediate destination was Ludd. Meantime the Colonel had returned from his reconnaissance, and after a scratch meal, during which we had a visit from Willie Law, we prepared once more to take the road and the camels were loaded up. Just as loading was starting a Turkish 'plane flew very low over the town and the camp, but fortunately did no damage.

The Brigade Column moved off sharp to time, and the convoy waited ready to follow. It was a long wait, and an hour and a half must have passed before we left the starting-point on the road near Ramleh Station. When we did eventually move we did so at a snail's pace, and checks were long and numerous. It was quite dark, and every little track which led on to the main road seemed choked with guns, ambulances or R.E. waggons, all making for the same route. The main road itself was literally packed with troops and transport, and the black dust peculiar to Ramleh floated along the column in dense clouds. Progress was so painfully slow that by the time we had turned up the road leading to Ludd it was midnight. The congestion was now so bad that further movement seemed almost hopeless, and to make matters more unpleasant, the night was cold and rain began to fall.

Affairs were quickly reaching the point of desperation when an order was passed down the column to halt till dawn and bivouac by the roadside. Now the road to Ludd is for the most part sunk below the level of the ground on either side, and as it is bordered by thick cactus hedges, the result was that most of the troops had to bivouac actually on the road. Since our time of starting at 7 p.m. we had taken five hours to cover less than one mile. Fortunately for us there was an open space at the side of the road opposite the convoy. It seemed once to have been a Turkish encampment, and was very badly cut up with holes, but we were able to find sufficient room to barrack and unload the camels. John Nicholl rode forward to find the Colonel and learn the arrangements for the next day. It was now raining heavily, and as

AMONG THE HILLS

bivouacs were not available, we had no protection of any kind. A cup of tea from M'Alpin, the Camel Officer, was the only bright spot in a most unpleasant night. Camel officers seem to move and have their being amid whatever comforts are possible, for M'Alpin's bivouac had been erected by his native servants, and tea was ready almost before our convoy was off the main road.

About 2 a.m. John Nicholl returned with the news that the Brigade would march again at 8 a.m., and that, as water and rations were to be drawn, the convoy must move forward at once to the Battalion, which lay about a mile further along the road. So there was nothing for it but to wake up the men, get the camels loaded and start away. To accomplish this in the dark and on very broken ground with some semblance of order was a job requiring considerable time and patience.

By 3.30 a.m. we had the camels arranged according to the Companies whose gear they carried, and moved out again on to the road. Progress was still very slow, as we had to thread our way among sleeping men, and often had to clear them to one side to allow room for the camels to pass. Fortunately the rain had stopped, and we reached the Battalion at 4.30 a.m. The Companies were lying in some gardens just to the right of the road, and a rough entrance had been cut through the cactus hedge.

The reason for the breakdown in the staff arrangements was apparently this: While lying at Ramleh the military situation in the hills had made it necessary to order the 156 and 157 Brigades forthwith to Ludd. The 157 Brigade was to proceed by the main road, which they took. The 156 Brigade was given a road which appeared on the map but which, unfortunately, did not exist on the ground. There was no time for reconnaissance of the routes, the unhappy result being that both Brigades were compelled to take the same road.

Ollernshaw was busy with rations and water, and by 7 a.m. both were issued to the troops and breakfasts were ready. For the convoy it was a strenuous night, and few of us had any chance to sit down, much less to sleep. Orders made it clear that we were now embarking on operations among the hills, and as it was necessary to move light, all packs were dumped in a Brigade Dump and left under guard. By 8 a.m. on the 19th November the Brigade was *en route*, and as soon as the camels were loaded we followed. Soon we passed through the village of Ludd, which, by the way, is the ancient Lydda, and contains the tomb of St. George, and striking off to the right, took the road which leads up to Jimzu. The village with this unmusical name stands on the shoulder of one of the foot hills, and the roughness of the road which leads to it gave us some foretaste of what was in store. For the first two hours we made excellent progress, but the going then became very difficult, and checks were numerous.

One lesson we thoroughly learned was to view with the gravest suspicion anything that was shown on the map as an "ancient Roman road." These at isolated points might be recognised for short stretches as rough and stony mountain tracks, but

AMONG THE HILLS

for the most part all signs of even a track had perished with the lapse of centuries, and they certainly proved a very poor advertisement to their ancient builders. During almost the entire day we climbed further and higher into the hills. The scenery was very rugged and wild, but we had struck a period of bad weather, and the day was dull. By 5 p.m. we found a guide waiting for us who had been left behind by the Battalion, and at a point about a mile short of Beit Likia we wheeled off to the left up a valley between two steep hillsides. We had still a considerable way to go, and it was nearly an hour later, and quite dark, when we eventually found Battalion Headquarters on a little rocky terrace beside a wall. Since leaving Ludd we had covered a distance of eighteen miles over the roughest possible ground. Rain was falling heavily, but my bivouac, which did duty as Battalion " Orderly Room," was soon pitched, and again took up its secondary rôle of Officers' Mess. On these occasions the rapidity with which a meal made its appearance was quite extraordinary, and very excellent meals they were.

The Companies were dotted round the hillsides on outpost duty, and must have spent a very uncomfortable night. The rain continued more or less till morning, but as I had had no sleep since leaving Ekron, it did not much affect my slumbers. On that night the 157 Brigade, which had followed on from Ludd, passed through us. On the forenoon of the 20th the Companies concentrated, and later the Battalion moved round the shoulder of the hill to an area near Brigade Headquarters, and not far from Beit Likia. I went on ahead with a small advance party to apportion the available space. It was no easy business to find any suitable bivouac area among these hills, for the entire surface was covered with stones and rocks, but we at last managed to secure a fairly level piece of ground at the mouth of the valley. Through this valley ran a wadi, and above its banks—about a quarter of a mile from our camp—there stuck up in the air the tail and wings of a wrecked Turkish aeroplane, which had apparently been shot down and nose-dived to its very rugged grave.

As night closed in rain again began to fall in torrents, and the air of the hills was cold. I was fortunate in having some sort of cover, for which I offered up many prayers of gratitude. Amid all these discomforts the spirits of the men were simply wonderful. They were still dressed in the thin khaki drill jackets and shorts which were well suited to the heat of the plains, but were not designed for hill fighting in the rainy season. We had no blankets nor greatcoats; the packs were all at Ludd, and the haversacks, which alone were left to carry any comforts, already contained an emergency ration and usually another day's ration in addition. Boots too were in many cases completely worn out with the hard marching and rough ground. It is no pleasant experience to spend an entire night cold and soaked to the skin, with no possibility of cover, but the more uncomfortable the conditions, the higher seemed to rise the spirits of the men. At three o'clock in the morning, while the rain was driving up the valley in solid

BRINGING UP THE GUNS INTO THE HILLS

AMONG THE HILLS

sheets, I saw them standing round in the glow cast by three fires, which they had lit from the branches of some almond trees, singing in chorus the popular songs of two years ago. Surely the result of the War was never really in doubt!

Fortunately with the return of daylight the weather cleared, and we spent a fairly comfortable and restful day.

At 1.30 a.m. on the 22nd we got orders for the Battalion to move at 5.30 a.m., so the night was somewhat disturbed. The convoy was to remain behind to await further orders, for it was doubtful if the transport could successfully negotiate the hill tracks which lay ahead. Just as day was dawning the Brigade marched off, and at 11 a.m. we were preparing to move with the convoy down to the main Jaffa-Jerusalem road to reach our destination *via* Enab, when the orders were changed, and eventually at 12.15 p.m. we followed with the camels by the route the Battalion had taken, and left the limbers behind at Likia. Very soon the road became a track, and the track a path, until all trace of it was lost on the stony hillsides. It was a good thing we had left the limbers behind, for camels were the only possible form of transport to cope with such conditions. At one point I saw some venturesome ambulance sand-carts drawn by mule teams, but they were making very heavy weather, for even with the most careful driving they were constantly jolting over rocks and into deep holes, and would have provided a very rough trip for any hospital cases they might have been carrying. One of our Batteries too was making a valiant effort to bring its guns along in the wake of the Infantry.

The spell of bad weather had now passed, and the scenery, as we climbed from hill to hill, was wild and grand. Away in the distance, through a gap, we could see the highest point crowned by the Mosque which marked our destination. It was the Mosque on Neby Samwil. As we halted in a narrow defile three enemy planes came over and provided us with a little anxiety, but our own airmen were very alert, and the Turkish planes, after taking a good look at us, passed quickly away to the north.

We knew very little of the general situation or of the immediate objects in view, but two facts were quite clear. First, that we were marching by the shortest route and with all speed toward Jerusalem ; and second, that our way lay directly across the enemy front. As a military manœuvre this seemed to contain considerable elements of risk, but it was not till later that we learned the stake for which we played. It seemed clear also that the movements in which we were now taking part were not the result of any long settled intention on the part of the Higher Command, but represented rather a gradual development of the situation. This development was influenced partly by the general direction of the Turkish retreat after the destruction of the Jaffa-Jerusalem railway ; partly by the fact that the troops of the 21st Corps were considerably in advance of the 20th Corps, and partly by the exploitation of local successes as we continued day by day to push our way further into the hills.

KUBEIBEH (EMMAUS) LOOKING EAST, WITH NEBY SAMWIL IN THE DISTANCE

AMONG THE HILLS

Roughly speaking, however, the plan, as finally worked out, was to give the enemy no breathing space, to allow him little opportunity to take advantage of the natural defences of the hills, and to push a stout wedge across the Jerusalem-Nablus road some miles to the north of Jerusalem. As a result of this, numbers of the enemy would find their line of retreat cut, and the Holy City would pass into our hands without subjecting it to the risk of damage by gun fire.

And so throughout the long afternoon we wound our way up into the hills, over passes and down into valleys, through narrow defiles, and always a higher ridge than the last pushed its way in front of us. Occasionally we could see the Yeomanry Patrols working out on our left flank toward the north. Away ahead there was plenty of activity, and the noise of guns came to us down the gentle breeze. The mantle of dusk descended, blotting out the distant view, and it was almost dark when we skirted the crest of a hill and found ourselves at Kubeibeh. There were one or two good solid stone buildings in the village, and toward one of them, which proved to be a Monastery now in use as a hospital, we saw a sad and weary string of wounded make their way. They were nearly all Native Indian troops of the 75th Division, but among them we found one or two of our own men. One with a wounded leg was helped along by a comrade who wore his arm in a sling; some were carried on stretchers; some limped along by themselves in little groups, and others were brought in cacolets carried by camels. The wounded were so numerous that the little road through the village was quite choked, and we were compelled to make a long halt. While the 52nd Division had come by Ramleh, Ludd and Beit Likia, the troops of the 75th Division had fought their way to Neby Samwil by the shorter route *via* the main Jerusalem road and Enab.

When eventually we came out on the other side of the village a cheerful hail in the voice of Steven Bilsland came to us out of the darkness. He had been waiting for the convoys, and was able to give us a little news. The Battalions were already spread out on a rough-and-ready line some two and a half miles ahead, near Neby Samwil, but they had been moving at dusk to other positions, and their present location was rather uncertain. A guide was provided for each Battalion's convoy, and our camels, with those of the 7th Scottish Rifles, were to leave the road about half a mile further on and strike out across country for Battalion Headquarters. The 7th Scottish Rifles' convoy, with Austin in charge, was directly ahead of our own, and as their guide did not materialise, we sent our man on to Austin at the head of the column, for both convoys were making for the same destination. Fortunately there was a moon, which made our job of finding the Battalion rather less hopeless.

Just before reaching Biddu we turned off the road to the left, and, skirting the shoulder of a hill, wound our way slowly over the rough ground and descended toward the valley. On many occasions we had to stop to find a way among the rocks, and as the convoy from both Battalions consisted of 150 camels, there was always the risk of the column

AMONG THE HILLS

breaking and those in the rear losing touch with those in front. It was a long, weary business, and as loads occasionally slipped and required adjustment, verbal messages rippled constantly up and down the column and checks were frequent. With the assistance of the small peep of moonlight we were able to pick out landmarks which might prove of use later on. The first of these was supplied by a group of thirty dead camels, which asserted their presence in a most noxious manner. Farther on we found all that remained of a dead Highlander —some shreds of tartan and two legs. Then a dead native Indian, and again a broken heap of iron rations. Such were the milestones on our road.

By 10 p.m. we reached a point near the place where our guide told us he had last seen the Battalion, but as there was now no sign of it, John Nicholl and I collected the camels together in a little open space and started out to find it. High up on a hillside, which seemed to be near the Mosque, we saw a streak of light which we decided to investigate. It was a longer journey than we expected, but in the end we were rewarded by finding the 7th Scottish Rifles with our own Battalion Headquarters on a rocky ledge near at hand. The locality seemed to be a particularly unhealthy one, and the Colonel told us we must bring the camels up and get them away again as soon as possible. So we trudged down the hill and back to where we had left the convoy. The men were all very weary and most of them sound asleep, but we soon got started again, and, finding some sort of a path, brought the camels to the foot of the hill below the ledge on which perched Battalion Headquarters. The ground near by was a perfect maze of little walled enclosures, but by breaking down the stones here and there we eventually reached a terrace where we could barrack the camels and unload the rations and water.

The Battalion had spent a most trying afternoon, for after being pushed up to Neby Samwil, they had been subjected to a perfect pounding from guns of all calibres, firing from the front and both flanks. In addition to this, the Turks were in force all round the Mosque on the crest of the hill, and at many points were within bombing distance of our own hastily-prepared defences. The enemy had apparently realised when too late that they had lost a key position, and were making every effort to regain it.

An hour later found us starting on the return journey to Kubeibeh, and after weary wanderings, which would have done credit to the Children of Israel, we struck the main road near Biddu at 3 a.m. Knowing that Brigade Headquarters were somewhere near, I found my way to Allan, the Staff Captain, and told him I would take our camels to a point off the road just east of Kubeibeh, where I thought reasonable cover might be obtained. And so we came to our journey's end, and by 5 a.m. on the 23rd the camels were off-loaded and our little camp was pitched. The "pitching" was a simple and speedy process, and consisted of rolling out our valises and getting inside them. We were all dog-tired, for since leaving Beit Likia we had been

TYPICAL SCENERY IN THE HILLS

constantly on the move for sixteen hours, with very little opportunity for food and none for rest.

About 6.30 a.m. I was awakened by the strong light in my eyes, and got up to look round. It did not take more than a very few seconds to impress on me the risks attached to selecting a suitable camping ground in the darkness, for daylight showed that we were in full view of the Turkish positions to the north. Ten minutes later this lesson was more thoroughly impressed on my mind when a shell landed right in the middle of the area. It was unfortunately followed immediately afterwards by many others, and one or two of the men were hit, while casualties occurred also among the camels. It seemed folly to remain in our present position, so I ordered an immediate move round a little shoulder, where a shallow re-entrant ran into the hillside. The men man-handled the baggage, and by 9 a.m. we were installed in our new position, and were able to have breakfast.

Lying handy was one of the walled enclosures which abound everywhere in the hills, and we were just arranging to place there the dumps for each Company and Battalion Headquarters when a 5.9 whined overhead and burst right in the middle of the enclosure. This was rather discouraging. Soon the shelling became almost constant, and the crash of the bursting H.E. reverberated among the rocks and echoed along the hillsides. No reply came from our own guns, as none had yet succeeded in making their way with us into the heart of the hills. We were able to obtain some cover under the lee of the numerous ledges and walls, but there was almost as much danger from the pieces of rock and stones which hurtled through the air as from the shells. The sun was very hot, and John Nicholl and I tried to gain a little shade by stretching my bivouac between the top of a ledge and the branches of a handy tree.

By midday Ollernshaw, who had taken some of the camels to Enab to draw rations, joined us again. He had gone *via* Biddu on one of the phantom Roman roads across the hills, and had been heavily shelled *en route*, but with good luck his party had escaped without casualties. In the early afternoon John Nicholl and I essayed a short sleep, but within five minutes of lying down at least twenty shells landed near by, and the bivouac stretched above us bellied in with the weight of stones and splinters of rock which fell on the top.

Again it seemed hopeless to remain in our present location, and when the shelling eased off a little John and I made our way along a wall to the main road with the object of finding other ground for our camp and camels, where rest at least might be a possibility. When we reached the corner of the Monastery garden we found James Austin. Allan had told him that he understood our Camp was in an excellent position, and that Austin should join us with the convoy of the 7th Scottish Rifles. With that object in view, Austin had come along to see where we were situated, but after watching the shelling to which we were being subjected, lost little time in deciding that it was hardly an ideal health resort ; that, in fact, it was a thoroughly undesirable camping area. We soon found a good

AMONG THE HILLS

piece of ground at the south-west corner of the Monastery garden, and arranged to move our Camp there after dusk.

As soon as the daylight had faded John and I got the camels loaded up with water and rations and set out for the Battalion, while Ollernshaw remained to move the Camp to its new position. It was a long weary trek, but our experiences of the previous night made the way easier, and by 10 p.m. we had climbed up the hill to Battalion Headquarters and safely handed over the rations and water. The officers at Battalion Headquarters looked distinctly war-worn. The Colonel was endeavouring to secure a short rest, while Dulieu, wearing a Balaclava helmet and two days' growth on his chin, was lying in his shack, with his message pad by his side. The Doctor, wrapped in a long waterproof cape which fell below his knees, arrived from his Aid Post, and Innes, looking like a first-rate criminal, was lying asleep, covered with several layers of his signal flags. Dick Coulson, as Mess President, was anxiously awaiting the arrival of the rations, for they had not yet dined. The day at Neby Samwil had been most unpleasant, for enemy shell fire had been continuous, while the complete silence of our own Artillery had not been a cheering feature. Casualties unfortunately had been numerous. In a few minutes after the arrival of the rations the cook produced an excellent stew, and as John and I had brought with us some medical comforts in the shape of two bottles of "Johnnie Walker," we had quite a cheerful meal.

At 11.30 p.m. we started on the return journey,

and passing such well-known landmarks as "Iron Ration Corner," "Dead Man Point," "Two Tree Hill," and "The Thirty Camels," we reached our new camping ground at 1.30 a.m. We had made the passage in good time, but journeys homeward are usually more rapid than those outward bound. I was thoroughly weary, and in a few seconds was inside my valise and asleep.

The 24th November at Kubeibeh was a comparatively restful day. We breakfasted late, and John and I went up to the Brigade Supply Dump to try to secure one or two candles, which were urgently required at Battalion Headquarters. The supply of these was practically nil, but we eventually managed to secure two, and considered ourselves very fortunate. We also succeeded in acquiring a few matches, which were more valuable than precious stones. Just to the west of Kubeibeh rises a little wooded hill crowned by gardens and a summer-house, to which a broad paved walk sweeps up from the village.

From the summit of the hill a wonderful view unfolds itself on all sides. Looking toward the west is the long series of rugged ridges and valleys which finally dip to the plain, until in turn the plain rolls itself out and reaches in the farthest distance the blue line of the Mediterranean. To the north is the boundless waste of hills, among which we could see the villages of Beit Dukka, Foka, and Beitunia. To the south the view is shut out by the ridge to the north of Enab. Our attention, however, was centred almost entirely on the east side, where Neby Samwil and its Mosque were almost hidden beneath the dust and smoke of bursting shells. The summit of Neby Samwil rises to some 2500 feet, and is the site of the ancient Mizpah, the fortress city of Benjamin. The Mosque covers the traditional tomb of the Prophet Samuel, and from its vantage point looks down on Jerusalem and the Mount of Olives, four miles distant.

Kubeibeh is the Emmaus of the New Testament, "which was from Jerusalem about three score furlongs." The Franciscan Monastery is said to stand over the spot where Christ broke bread with the two disciples. The Monastery garden is large and peaceful, with beautiful trees and many water courses, and is tended with affectionate care by the long-robed Monks. One of the Lowland Field Ambulances had made its temporary home among its trees, and not far away another large building—which had been a German Catholic Hospice—was now a very efficient hospital, with the Red-Cross flag fluttering from its roof.

As we watched the storm of shell-fire which blotted out the Mosque from view, our men were engaged in their gallant but forlorn task of forcing the Jib-Nebala-Hannina line and the north road to Nablus. To ensure success strong forces were required, but unfortunately the toll of war had been heavy, and the 52nd Division was now little more than a shadow of its former self, while the greater part of the enemy forces was composed of fresh troops who had not been engaged around Gaza or during the period of the pursuit. With the exception of the 75th Division, which was now very weak in numbers, there were no other troops available to support the attack, and in spite of all its determination and gallantry the 52nd Division was unable to carry through a task which was so hopelessly beyond its powers. A few of our guns had now been able to make their way through the hills, but their contribution to the general chorus was pathetically insufficient.

At dusk we again made our way to the Battalion. It had been a bad day, and the spirits of the little party on the ledge at Battalion Headquarters were rather subdued. A rumour that the Battalion was to be relieved that night proved false, and instead of relief the 156 Brigade was ordered to take over the line of the 234 Brigade (75th Division), in addition to the section it already held. Casualties all over had been heavy, and the ration strength of " Y " Company, which had been most heavily hit, had dropped to twenty-three. When we made our way down the hill I saw in the darkness a vast shallow grave which had been scraped in the stony ground, and here some fifty of our men found rest from the fight.

On the morning of the 25th November we heard the cheering news that the 60th Division was at hand, and that we would be relieved that night. The Brigade was to go to Beit Anan—a village which lay a couple of miles behind Kubeibeh—and there to rest for two days until the whole Division moved down to the plain. In the forenoon John and I visited Carswell, who had been wounded on the previous day and was now in the German Hospice. He had been shot through the knees,

AMONG THE HILLS

and his journey by cacolet from Battalion Headquarters had been a hazardous one. At dusk John Nicholl and Ollernshaw took sufficient camels to move the Battalion's baggage, etc., from Neby Samwil, and I, with the remainder, set out later on with rations and water for Beit Anan to have things ready when the Battalion arrived. The ground allotted to us at Beit Anan was merely part of a hillside, but we were able to find reasonable space for the Companies and Battalion Headquarters on the rocky terraces.

The cook fires were soon going, and a meal was ready when the first of the Companies arrived just as day dawned on the 26th. There was not an officer or man who was not absolutely worn out from physical exhaustion, and the craving for sleep was stronger even than hunger, for many lay down and slept without waiting for food. Ferguson and Westland arrived with the handful of men which represented "Y" Company, and the Colonel and Dulieu followed with Battalion Headquarters. The Battalion and the whole Brigade had passed through a most searching and fiery ordeal, and emerged weary and with sadly thinned ranks, but with undiminished spirit.

On this day a camel convoy for the Division came up from the plain, and some thoughtful Postal Officer sent up with it several bags of mail and some parcels. They arrived just at the psychological moment. Since leaving Gaza we had received no mail, so home letters were more than an ordinary treat, while the parcels afforded a break in the monotony of bully beef and biscuits, which had been almost our only rations since the pursuit began. Bully beef can be an excellent dish when taken at reasonable intervals, but when it is called into service at least twice a day for three weeks familiarity is apt to breed if not contempt, at least a strong craving for change of menu. Army biscuits too are an excellent and sustaining diet, but too prolonged an encounter with their unrelenting substance usually entails heavy casualties to one's dental arrangements.

In the evening I dined with Humble and Allan Rogers, who were now the only officers remaining with "W" Company. I had certainly anticipated nothing more than the usual ration fare, but an excellent meal arrived, consisting of Soup, Lobster, Pie, Fruit and Savoury, accompanied on its way by Whisky, Port and Coffee. Considering all the circumstances, it was a great achievement even for "W" Company.

The 27th November was a very restful day, and arrangements were made for the Brigade to set out on the following morning *en route* for Ramleh. In the forenoon Steven Bilsland and I inspected the village and inhabitants of Beit Anan. It is a very dirty place, composed of loosely built stone hovels, which usually are more suggestive of dug-outs than dwelling-houses, and its people are not attractive. The few men we saw looked a useful class of brigand, and the women, clad in garments of a dirty red colour, sat outside the houses crushing grain in stone urns.

During the afternoon we learned that the Yeomanry on the hills round Foka had been forced

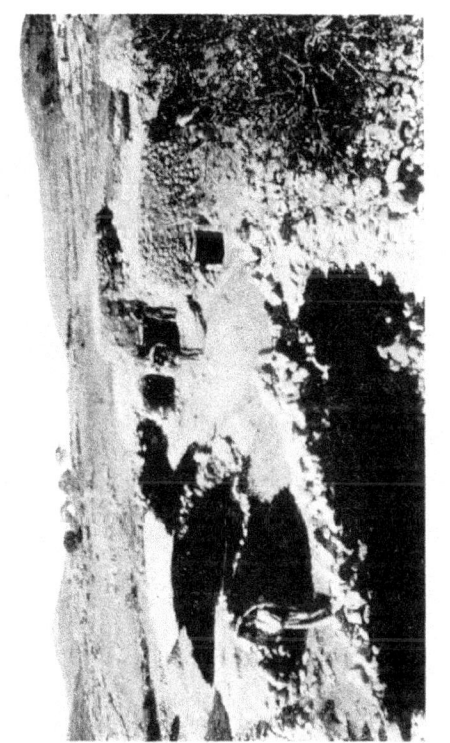

NATIVE DWELLINGS AT BEIT ANAN
156 Brigade Bivouac in distance

AMONG THE HILLS

back, and to the north we could see the bursts of the Turkish shells following them along the ridge. There was a heavy feeling of apprehension in the air, and we wondered if after all our present spell of fighting was really over. However, no counter orders reached us, and at 9 a.m. on the morning of the 28th the Brigade moved off. The Convoys which were brigaded, followed immediately behind. Shells were now bursting within a few hundred yards of our bivouac area, and there seemed to be every chance that our stay among the hills might be prolonged. About half an hour later we could see from our place in the convoy that the road in front was receiving the attention of the Turkish gunners, and it soon became quite apparent that we would not pass unmolested. After descending a hillside we reached the danger spot, and as the shelling of the road was very accurate, we decided to move the convoy a little way off the path and send the camels round in batches by a short detour, which would bring them again to the road a little farther on. It was at this point that a certain Staff Officer, whose experience of camels cannot have been very profound, enquired impatiently why we did not make the camels trot! Of such are the humours of war.

Some casualties had already been claimed among the Infantry, and one or two dead horses and mules were lying by the roadside, but by good luck we got safely past without losses, and half a mile farther on the convoy was able to close up again and carry on. It was an anxious half hour. During the days we had spent at Neby Samwil the

Pioneer Companies of the Division had effected an extraordinary improvement in the state of the roads, so we were able to make good progress.

At Beit Likia we picked up our limbers which we had left there on the 22nd, and when we reached the open ground a little farther to the west we found that the whole Brigade had halted there, a fact which seemed ominous. When we reached the Battalion it appeared quite definite that we must once more take to the hills and help to prevent the enemy breaking our lateral line of communication. In the early afternoon we received orders to move with the Brigade to a point just to the north of the village of Beit Sira. The Convoy followed immediately behind the Battalion, and in less than an hour we had passed Beit Sira and entered a wide valley with low hills on either side. The valley gradually narrowed until it was almost closed in by a low semi-circular ridge of the usual rocks and stones. Here we relieved the 155 Brigade, which had preceded us from the hills and had been holding in check the Turkish turning movement on our left flank. On the reverse slope of the ridge Battalion Headquarters made its home.

The Turks were obviously in some force near by, for as we made our way to Battalion Headquarters a constant shower of bullets whizzed overhead and cracked among the rocks. A Turkish mountain-gun endeavoured to get the range of our road, but fortunately most of the shells fell wide. It seemed our fate to be sent on most unpleasant jobs with an entire absence of Artillery support, for here again not a gun lifted its voice from our

AMONG THE HILLS

side. By the time we had handed over the rations and water the engagement was quite brisk and the Doctor was busy. Bill Roger of the M.G.C., who was attached to us, was helped down to Battalion Headquarters with a bullet in his leg, and was soon off on the long trail which would lead, with luck, to Cairo.

Meantime we had sent the camels back to a point near the village where we could obtain some cover and be handy for supplies. Our spirits were not at the brightest, and as we walked back together John was almost pessimistic. He had just finished explaining fully the unusual dangers and unpleasant possibilities of the military situation when, with a terrific crack, a salvo of 18-pounder shells fired from a Battery behind the village whizzed overhead into Turkey-land. The effect was electrical and immensely cheering to everyone, and by the time we reached our little camp it was a confirmed optimist who walked by my side. The Battery which had arrived so opportunely belonged to another Division, and was soon followed by other Batteries.

John and I made our temporary home in a little stone sangar like a diminutive walled-in sheep-pen, over which I stretched my bivouac, and before going to sleep we disposed of one of the parcels which had reached me at Beit Anan, and which contained such luxuries as sardines, peaches, cream, and sweet biscuits. Supplies of tobacco had long since run out, and our smokes were very few and far between. If anyone was lucky enough to be possessed of any matches, they were handed over as a point of duty to the cooks for lighting the fires. During the next two days our routine was much the same as at Neby Samwil, and each evening we walked up to Battalion Headquarters with the rations. St. Andrew's day would probably have passed unnoticed had it not been for a special message accompanied by a very precious gift in the shape of a bottle of whisky which reached Battalion Headquarters from the Brigadier. While at Beit Sira Dick Coulson left us to take over command of the 5th K.O.S.B.

On 1st December the 10th (Irish) Division was at hand, and orders were issued for our relief on that night. In the evening I moved off with a small advance party to a bivouac area about two miles farther back, by the side of the road leading to Kubab. After dark the Battalion was relieved by the 5th Royal Inniskilling Fusiliers, and by 11 p.m. the 8th Scottish Rifles arrived and settled down for the night in our new area. We were very much struck by the freshness and numerical strength of the Divisions which had relieved us at Neby Samwil and Beit Sira, for each of their Battalions appeared to be stronger than our entire Brigade.

We now felt that our arduous days among the hilltops had really come to an end, but the natural feeling of relief was tinged with more than a suspicion of regret. No one wanted more fighting, but during all the days of the advance, and even amid the miseries of Neby Samwil, the excitement of the chase was on everyone, and Jerusalem —the *spolia opima*—lay ahead. And then, after

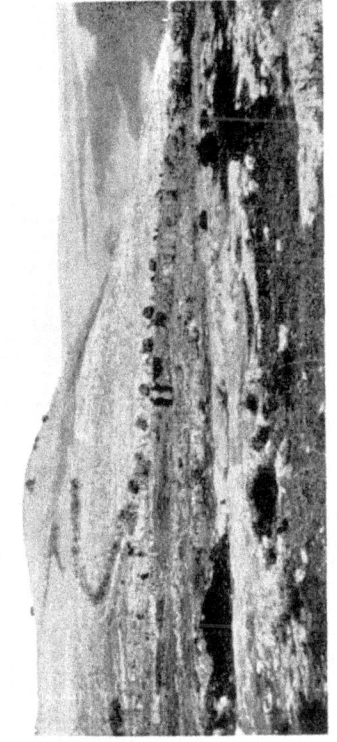

156 BRIGADE COLUMN LEAVING BEIT ANAN

AMONG THE HILLS

looking down on the Mount of Olives and the domes and spires of the Holy City, when the prize seemed almost within our reach, the final task was handed over to fresher and numerically stronger Divisions for completion. Without doubt they would in the end attain the goal toward which we had marched and fought, and our only witnesses among these wild hills would be the good comrades whom we had left sleeping beside the little wooden crosses under the deep shadow of Neby Samwil.

On the following morning we prepared for the next stage in our wanderings, which was to take us to Kubab, and the whole Brigade marched off at 12.30 p.m. I rode on ahead with Bruce Allan to arrange our bivouac area. It was a lovely day, and as we passed out from the hills, with all their unpleasant memories, and moved out on the Jerusalem-Jaffa road, life suddenly seemed to become more care-free and happy. Kubab is a native village standing on a bluff by the roadside, and gains whatever charm it may possess from the setting of olive gardens in which it is placed. I was allotted a number of these gardens in which to bivouac the Battalion, and it would have been difficult to find a more beautiful spot.

The route followed by the Brigade was only some five miles in length, and the Battalion arrived at 3 p.m. Like so many of these gardens and enclosures, it was difficult to find anything in the way of an entrance, but the Battalion Pioneers, armed with entrenching tools and led on by Sergeant M'Robbie, carried out a determined attack on a wall and some shrubs, with the result that in ten minutes the Battalion had passed through and settled down among the trees. It was delightful to lie down on ground that was soft and level and leafy, without nasty angular stones and rocks denting one's recumbent form. This was certainly the most peaceful night we had spent since leaving Gaza, and our imaginations carried us forward to such wonderful luxuries as a big home mail, a good wash and clean clothes, tobacco, cigarettes, fresh meat and bread.

At 10.15 a.m. on 3rd December I again rode forward in advance to find the area near Ramleh, where we hoped to have a few days of complete rest. We passed along by the main road, and six miles farther on crossed the railway at Ramleh Station. The town was looking just as dirty as on our previous visit, and we were glad that our camping ground lay clear of it, two miles ahead on the rolling country near the little village of Surafend. The Battalion arrived at 3 p.m., and the Companies were spread out over a large grassy slope. On the following day the Transport brought us our packs, which, a fortnight earlier, had been dumped at Ludd, and very shortly our home mails, clean clothes, tobacco and rations materialised.

Our arrival at Ramleh closed a very complete and crowded phase of the operations, so far as the 52nd Division was concerned. Up till the 6th November it was never intended or expected that we should take any part in the pursuit, but, in effect, along with the 75th Division and detachments of the Cavalry, we had borne the entire

AMONG THE HILLS

brunt of the operations from Gaza to the very threshold of Jerusalem. Long and wearisome marches, undertaken sometimes in the scorching heat of the sands and sometimes in the piercing cold and rain of the hills, followed immediately by stiff engagements, became almost the daily routine. The supply of rations and water was a constant and intense anxiety, and daily, as railhead receded from us, these difficulties became more acute. Without doubt the finest thing of all during these crowded weeks was the spirit of our men. There are no grander fellows in the world.

The following is an extract from General Sir Edmund Allenby's Official Despatch, which covers the period of our fighting among the hills:

"On the 19th the Infantry commenced its advance. One portion was to advance up the main road as far as Kuryet el Enab, with its right flank protected by Australian mounted troops. From that place, in order to avoid any fighting in the close vicinity of the Holy City, it was to strike north towards Bireh by a track leading through Biddu. The remainder of the infantry was to advance through Berfilya to Beit Likia and Beit Dukka, and thence support the movement of the other portion.

After capturing Latron and Amwas on the morning of the 19th, the remainder of the day was spent in clearing the defile up to Saris, which was defended by hostile rearguards.

On the 20th Kuryet el Enab was captured with the bayonet in the face of organised opposition, while Beit Dukka was also captured. On the same day the Yeomanry got to within four miles of the Nablus-Jerusalem road, but were stopped by strong opposition about Beitunia.

On the 21st a body of infantry moved north-east by a track from Kuryet el Enab through Biddu and Kulundia towards Bireh. The track was found impassable for wheels, and was under hostile shell-fire. Progress was slow, but by evening the ridge on which stands Neby Samwil was secured. A further body of troops was left at Kuryet el Enab to cover the flank and demonstrate along the main Jerusalem road. It drove hostile parties from Kustul, $2\frac{1}{2}$ miles east of Kuryet el Enab, and secured this ridge.

By the afternoon of the 21st advanced parties of Yeomanry were within two miles of the road and an attack was being delivered on Beitunia by other mounted troops.

The positions reached on the evening of the 21st practically marked the limit of progress in this first attempt to gain the Nablus-Jerusalem road. The Yeomanry were heavily counter-attacked and fell back, after bitter fighting, on Beit ur el Foka (Upper Bethoron). During the 22nd the enemy made two counter-attacks on the Neby Samwil ridge, which were repulsed. Determined and gallant attacks were made on the 23rd and on the 24th on the strong positions to the west of the road held by the enemy, who had brought up reinforcements and numerous machine-guns, and could support his infantry by artillery fire from guns placed in positions along the main road. Our artillery, from lack of roads, could not be brought up to give adequate support to our infantry. Both attacks failed, and it was evident that a period of preparation and organisation would be necessary before an attack could be delivered in sufficient strength to drive the enemy from his positions west of the road.

Orders were accordingly issued to consolidate the positions gained and prepare for relief.

Though these troops had failed to reach their final objectives, they had achieved invaluable results. The narrow passes from the plain to the plateau of the Judean range have seldom been forced, and have been fatal to many invading armies. Had the attempt not been made at once, or had it been pressed with less determination, the enemy would have had time to reorganise his defences in the passes lower down, and the conquest of the plateau would then have been slow, costly, and precarious. As it was, positions had been won from which the final attack could be prepared and delivered with good prospects of success."

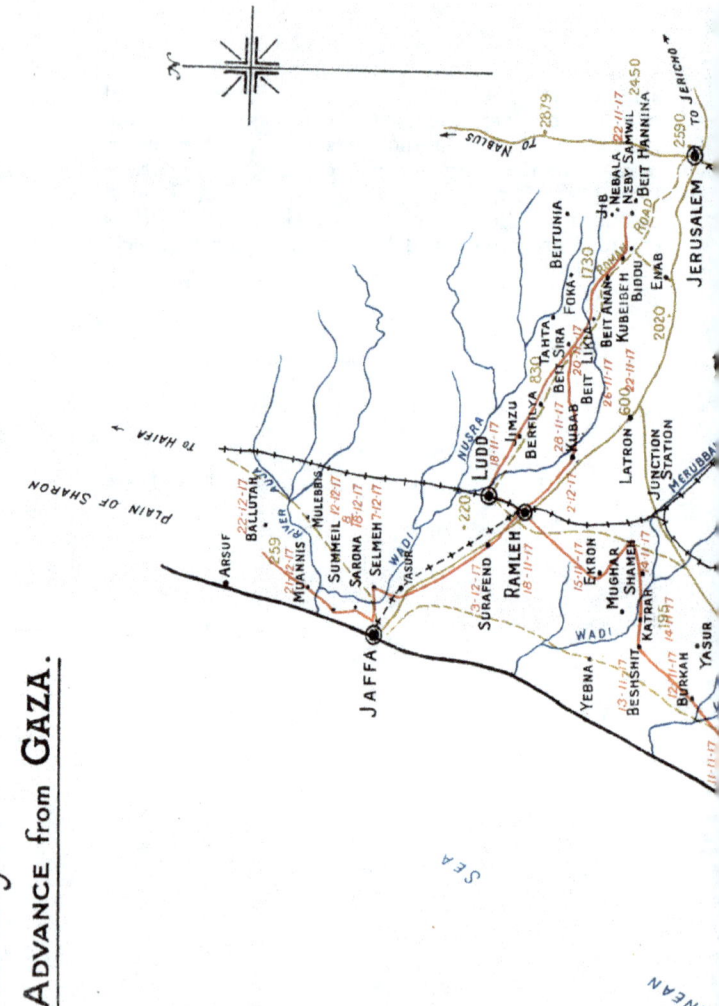

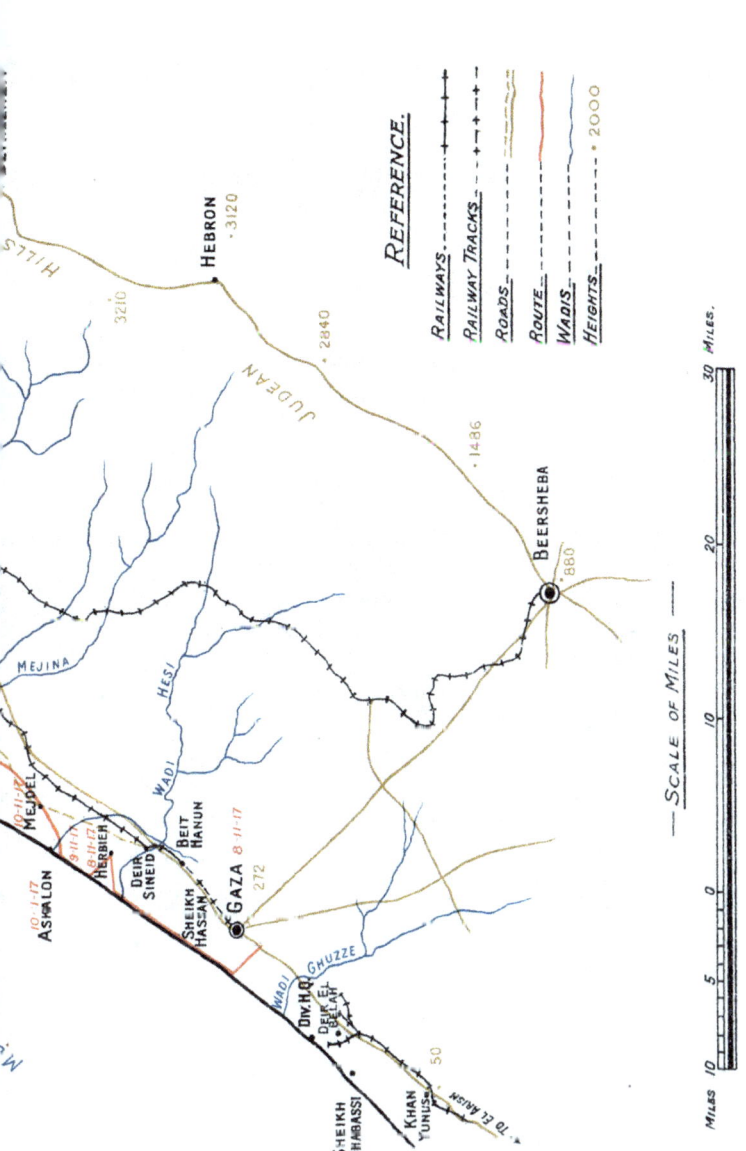

IN THE LAND OF THE ORANGE GROVES

ADVENTURES WITH A WADI AND SOME CAMELS—SARONA AND ITS ORANGE GROVES—THE FORCING OF THE AUJA—ON THE PLAIN OF SHARON—EXPECTATIONS AND REALITIES OF CHRISTMAS EVE IN THE HOLY LAND—HOW TO CONDUCT AN ALARM WITH FULL SCENIC EFFECT.

THE days at Surafend were very restful. We were able to get plenty of water for washing our bodies and our clothes, and the bivouac areas were gay with lines of blankets, shirts, socks, etc., drying in the sun. We succeeded also in getting most of the men fitted out with new service-dress uniforms, but best of all were the new boots, of which we received quite a good supply. On 6th December we received orders to move on the following day to an area near Selmeh, a village lying some eight miles nearer Jaffa and about one and a half miles north of the main Jerusalem-Jaffa road.

Unfortunately after our spell of sunshine at Surafend the weather broke, and early in the forenoon of the 7th just as heavy rain had begun to fall, I was ordered to meet the Staff Captain at 11.15 a.m. at Selmeh, and I set out from the

THE LAND OF ORANGE GROVES

bivouac area at 10. It was not a pleasant ride, as the rain continued in torrents and the road resembled a river in flood. At Yasur I turned off the main road along a rough track over the open country, and soon afterwards crossed the embankment of the meter gauge line which connects Ramleh with Jaffa. There were no rails, as these had been lifted by the Turks for the construction of a branch line near Gaza.

A little further on a deep broad wadi gaped wide in front. It ran at right angles to my route, and although at one point some attempt had been made by the gunners to cut a rough road through the banks, the crossing at that time for anything but horses or camels would not have been easy. The banks were roughly twenty feet high, and the soft mud at the sides and in the bed had become greasy and slippery with the rain. Soon after negotiating the wadi I met Bruce Allan and John Tulloch near the outskirts of Selmeh, and a little later was shown the area where the Battalion would bivouac on arrival. As the downpour of rain was continuous and as there was no shelter near by, I accompanied Bruce Allan to Jaffa on a quest for lunch. The track led right through the orange groves for some three miles, and after crossing the Iron Bridge which carries the road over a deep wadi, we entered the outskirts of the town. It was pleasant to see substantial houses again, and we soon found our way to Hardegg's Jerusalem Hotel. Business seemed somewhat dislocated, for after a long wait the most meagre of lunches appeared. The only vegetable was a curious concoction which seemed to be composed principally of song bird seed. Rations were small, and the edge of our hunger was hardly dulled by the time an eggcup-ful of Turkish coffee proclaimed the meal at an end.

By 3 p.m. I was back at the main road at Yasur, where I met the Battalion advance party, which had brought with it sufficient camels to carry rations, water, and the cooks' gear. When we reached the wadi I found that its condition had become much worse with the rain, and it was only after long delay and by crossing at a very wide angle at a point where some long coarse grass on the banks gave a precarious foothold for the camels that we found ourselves all safe on the other side. Then we pushed on to the bivouac area, and got things ready for the arrival of the Battalion. I was glad to find that Pryer had brought my bivouac and valise on one of the camels, so I had at least the cheering expectation of dry clothing. Our idea as to the exact whereabouts of the enemy was not very clear, but we were warned to avoid certain points which fell under his observation, and the bivouac area was arranged on the rear slope of some rising ground. Rain continued steadily, and when darkness closed down it was accompanied by a biting wind. The Brigade was not to reach Yasur until after dark, as it was not considered advisable to have large bodies of troops moving by daylight along the main road and exposed to aircraft observation and possible bombing.

About 5.30 p.m. I set out again on my horse with the object of meeting the Battalion at the wadi and guiding it to the Bivouac area. To help

THE LAND OF ORANGE GROVES 121

the Battalions to reach their respective areas in the dark and over the open country Norris Haugh, the Brigade Intelligence Officer, had established a chain of posts, each composed of a couple of men, leading forward from the wadi, and I essayed to make my way back along the chain. Unfortunately I must have passed through between two of the links, and it was no easy job to hit the wadi and find the crossing. The ground was almost a quagmire, and was broken here and there by smaller wadis. Eventually I succeeded in finding the crossing, and along with my horse literally slid down the greasy side into the wadi bed. We were in process of stumbling up the other bank when a torch shone out of the darkness, and I was hailed by Colonel Findlay. The Brigadier and Colonel Peebles had preceded the Brigade on a reconnaissance, so the Colonel was in Command of the Brigade, and I had struck the head of the column. Captain Sayer, the new Brigade Major, whose appointment had followed Captain Franklin's death at Kubeibeh, was with him.

I reported on the condition of the wadi, and it was decided that the crossing was then out of the question for wheeled transport, but that the camels might make the attempt. Steven Bilsland was in charge of the Brigade limbers, which followed immediately behind the infantry, and I made my way along the column to tell him to take them back to a point near the main road at Yasur. The rain continued to descend in torrents and the night was inky black.

After finding Steven, I went further back to see

how John Nicholl was faring with the camels. Every man in the Brigade column had long since been soaked to the skin; marching in the deep mud was a weariness and toil, and conditions generally were pure misery, but the difficulties of the men were as nothing compared to the lot of the camels. Their state was simply pitiable. The passage of the Infantry and limbers had increased the hopeless condition of the ground, which had become one vast sea of watery mud and slime. There was no foothold for the camels, and they staggered and slipped and fell in all directions. Ropes broke and loads collapsed, and when once barracked to readjust the load, it was almost impossible to coax a beast again to its feet. Our experiences in the hills had bred in us a great admiration for the powers and prowess of the camels, and it was pathetic to see their plight. At intervals a camel, slipping in the mud, would find its forelegs slide from under it, and with its struggles to rise again only became more deeply embedded in the mire.

Amid these difficulties the men who accompanied the camels worked with the greatest patience and endurance to make progress easier, and literally step by step the beasts were shepherded across the railway embankment and over the open ground to the wadi. Later I was told of camels belonging to other units which had withstood all the cold and rain of the hills only to find a grave in the mud of this night. Some three hours were spent in covering no more than three hundred yards. But in spite of all, there still remained a last flickering

THE LAND OF ORANGE GROVES

hope that with care and luck we might be able to achieve a crossing and reach the Battalion, which long since had vanished into the darkness.

Buffeted by the wind and rain, John Nicholl and I ploughed our way through the mud at the edge of the wadi in the vain hope that we might find some part where the ground had been less churned up by the passage of the troops. At one point, when John was walking half a pace in front of me, he suddenly disappeared, and the ground seemed to have swallowed him up. In reality he had merely fallen over the edge of the wadi, and a moment or two later his voice hailed me from the depths. In a little while he succeeded in climbing up the side and, thickly encased in mud, joined me again. Our clothes since early in the afternoon had given up the attempt to keep any part of our bodies dry, and a very persistent little cold stream trickled down the small of my back. Reluctantly we decided that it was quite hopeless to attempt to negotiate the wadi until, with the return of dawn, might come the chance of a lift in the weather or the opportunity of a detour by an easier route.

At 2 a.m., not being able to help further but feeling rather that I was deserting a ship in distress, I left John and pushed on to the Battalion. My horse was a clever old beast, and together we slithered down the wadi bank and struggled up the other side. It was an hour later when I skirted the fringe of cactus hedge at the north of the village, and on hailing the Battalion I was very relieved to hear an answering shout from the darkness. I felt sure that the noble Pryer would have my bivouac erected, and I looked forward to the dry clothes reposing in my valise. These expectations, however, were realised only in part, for I found that my bivouac was already tenanted by nine officers, several of whom were soundly sleeping in a confused heap on the top of my valise. With difficulty I was able to insinuate myself among the tangle of legs into an atmosphere reeking with wet clothing but pleasantly warm, and I was still in time for the remains of a supper consisting of cold "Maconachie" and water. As it was almost impossible to move even a cramped limb much less to deal with one's wardrobe, the dream of dry clothes did not materialise till many hours later. The last five weeks had provided an unrivalled assortment of experiences, but for pure and undiluted misery the palm must undoubtedly pass to the night at the wadi at Selmeh.

Early in the morning of the 8th the rain subsided to a drizzle, and John Nicholl, who had managed by taking a detour to find an easier way across the wadi, succeeded in reaching the Battalion with his camels complete. We were in process of cleaning up when I received orders to set out again with the Staff Captain for Sarona.

We took the road through the groves which we had used on the previous day, and passing the outskirts of Jaffa, we rode into Sarona at 1 p.m. The village, which stands on slightly rising ground about a mile and a half north-east of Jaffa, had become a thriving German-Jewish colony. Although the day was thoroughly wet and the sun refused to shine, the first sight of its neat little

A BYE-WAY IN SARONA

THE LAND OF ORANGE GROVES

street, with creeper-clad houses and luxurious foliage, afforded a very pleasant surprise. I had left Selmeh expecting at the journey's end to be apportioned the usual bare and uninteresting bivouac area in the open, but instead of that I was handed over six solid houses with their outbuildings in which to billet the Battalion. The men of the village had already been removed and interned, and the German womenfolk were now busy moving their furniture into the two locked rooms left at their disposal in each house or moving portions of their household goods in crazy carts to the district allotted to them in Jaffa. Many of the outhouses were commodious, and head-cover at least was obtainable for every man of the Battalion.

When the Brigade arrived about 3 p.m. two of the Battalions passed right through the village to take over the positions on the south bank of the river Auja, and considering the state of the weather, we felt more than lucky that the lot of the Battalion for the next few days would be cast in comparative comfort. Battalion Headquarters settled down in house No. 41, and after showing the Companies to their billets, I had the satisfaction of a hot bath in a large tin tub and a complete change of clothing. It was a great treat to sleep once more on a bed, and life in general became more cheerful. Rain fell steadily all during the next day, and the constant traffic along the little streets had whipped their surface into deep soft mud. Most of the day was spent in improving the billeting arrangements, taking inventories of furniture, and sending beds and bedding from the different houses to the Field Ambulance, which had established itself temporarily in the village hall.

On the 10th the sun again shone forth with all its brilliance, the ground quickly began to dry and conditions became more pleasant. Dulieu, who had certainly missed his vocation as a landscape gardener, was busily superintending a party engaged in beautifying the surroundings of Battalion Headquarters. With the return of good weather it seemed now possible to appreciate more fully the beauties of the village, and in the dancing sunlight it presented a very picturesque appearance. The village itself lies in the midst of orange gardens and plantations, and appears to have been laid out originally in the shape of a cross. As additional houses were added this idea became less easy to retain, but the plan of the cross is still clearly shown in the two roads which intersect at the north of the village near the hall. The houses for the most part are fashioned of wood, but there are one or two good substantial dwellings of stone. Pigeons in dozens cooed their songs from among the eaves.

A large Distillery provided a light red wine of the claret variety, with some fiery spirit to which the name of brandy was given, and part of the Distillery building was soon transformed into a very efficient bathing establishment. To each house was attached its little garden, and the roads were fringed with trees. Many of the houses were festooned with creepers, and little purple, blue and red flowers peeped out from among the greenery and filled the side-walks with their perfume. The

THE LAND OF ORANGE GROVES

orange groves approached to within a few yards of the houses, and the trees hung heavily with thick clusters of bright yellow fruit. The wonderfully fragrant scent from the groves filled the evening air as with a breath from dreamland. Looking past the orange gardens from the windows of our house, a belt of rough ground lay almost covered by a tangle of vine branches, and further on the sand dunes stretched down to meet the blue sparkle of the Mediterranean. A little to the south white roofs raised their heads from among the gardens and palm trees of Jaffa. It was all very pretty and restful.

Meantime the Turk had maintained himself in a position on the high ground just north of the river Auja, which flows into the sea some 3000 yards north of Sarona, and from his vantage point was able to keep observation on Jaffa and the intervening ground. It was whispered that the next job for the Division would be to dislodge him from his present position and drive him north across the Plain of Sharon. A few shells landed each day in Sarona, just to remind us of his presence, but although one shell actually pierced the roof of a house where a Regimental M.O. was engaged with his sick parade, little damage resulted.

On the 12th we were due to take our turn in the front line, and as soon as it became dusk the Companies moved out to their different posts, while Battalion Headquarters took up residence in the best house in the little scattered village of Summeil. This village was about half a mile nearer the river, and many of its houses were almost completely hidden among the orange gardens. By this time we had become rather particular and critical as to the quality of oranges, but I have certainly never tasted finer fruit than hung from the trees just outside the walls of Battalion Headquarters. The days at Summeil were pleasant and for the most part uneventful. The weather was good, and the trenches held by our posts became more habitable and less like young canals.

Meantime preparations and plans for the forcing of the Auja and the capture of the commanding position on the north bank went on apace. The Auja, next to the Jordan, is the largest river in Palestine, and its course lay directly across our front. Its breadth of forty yards and depth of ten feet rendered it an obstacle of first-class importance, and the one bridge which crossed the river at some miles from its mouth had already been severely damaged. Here was a military undertaking of the greatest difficulty and complexity, and I believe I am correct in saying that to the credit of Brigadier-General A. H. Leggett stands, in the first instance, the formulation of the plans which later on were crowned with such success. It was obvious that to cross a river of the importance of the Auja and attack strong enemy positions on the other side by daylight was next to impossible, so it was decided that the operation should be carried out by night. All three Brigades of the Division were to be employed, and the first problem was the method by which the troops could be transported in safety and silence to the other side without any inkling of our plans becoming apparent to the enemy. The

PONTOON BRIDGE ACROSS THE AUJA

THE LAND OF ORANGE GROVES 129

157 Brigade was to cross by the ford which was known to exist near the mouth of the river; the 156 Brigade was to cross over almost directly in front of Summeil, while the 155 Brigade was to make use of the stone bridge further to the east.

One evening Lieut.-Colonel James Anderson of the 6th H.L.I., with three other officers, called at Battalion Headquarters at Summeil. He left us as dusk was closing in to carry out a reconnaissance of the ford. It was an unusual and very hazardous venture, for after reaching the beach a few hundred yards south of the river mouth he entered the water and, accompanied by another officer, swam along until he reached the channel of the river and found the ford. Depths at various points were accurately measured, and sticks were placed in the water showing the exact direction which must be followed by the troops. And this work was successfully completed literally under the muzzles of Turkish machine-guns on the other side. This exploit won for Colonel Anderson a bar to his D.S.O.

The problem of the crossing of our own Brigade was even more difficult, for there was no ford of any kind, and to make matters worse, the rains had swollen the river to full flood. A bridge or flat-bottomed boats supplied the only solution, and it was necessary to place the bridge at some point which might escape immediate detection by the enemy. To this end the most careful and constant observation was kept on enemy movements and posts, and a very useful and risky reconnaissance was made during darkness by Stanley Smith of the 7th Scottish Rifles, who, under cover of night, crossed the river in a small pontoon with the object of noting any enemy activity on the other bank. His crossing was unnoticed by the enemy; soundings of the river were taken and much valuable information gained.

The success of the plans for our crossing now rested largely with the Engineers. They decided first to prepare a Pontoon Bridge, which could quickly be thrown across the river and the sections of which could meantime be got ready and hidden among the bushes near the south bank. In addition to the bridge a number of flat-bottomed boats were also prepared, with rope attachments for pulling the craft backwards and forwards across the river with the minimum noise and loss of time. Even assuming the success of the preparations for the actual crossing, it was obvious that the entire success or failure of the whole operation must depend finally on the steadiness and silence of the troops. Another factor of prime importance was the state of the weather on the night of the attack. The spongy low ground near the river was already soft and muddy, which would render the passage of troops difficult, while a night sufficiently dark to help in preventing the detection of our plans by the enemy would present a compensating difficulty in keeping touch and direction when the other bank was reached.

So much for the general plans for the crossing, but these, while so all-important, were merely the prelude to the subsequent attack on the Turkish positions. Careful observations had shown that the enemy line on the north side was not a continuous one, but was composed of a number of

THE LAND OF ORANGE GROVES 131

strong posts placed in commanding tactical positions, and our dispositions were made with the object of pushing columns of the attacking forces round these posts, so that they could be dealt with from the flanks or rear. The plans were framed with a thoroughness and detail which seemed to provide for all contingencies, but a night operation of such difficulty and magnitude demanded also that luck should range itself on the side of the 52nd Division.

On the night of the 18th December our Battalion was relieved by the New Zealand Auckland Mounted Rifles (dismounted for the occasion), and came back for two days' rest to Sarona. It was seldom in Palestine that Cavalry was called upon for duty in the trenches, and the Canterbury Mounted Rifles were certainly unused to the methods and formalities of taking over a stretch of the line. Their advance party consisted of two Squadron Leaders, and when they were taken up to the front posts and met our Company Commanders they mentioned casually that our Companies could safely go now, as their Boys would be along in a little while. There was quite a freshness in the idea, but it was altogether too novel for a staid Infantry Battalion, and our Companies remained in position until the relieving troops were actually in the trenches.

Parts of the following days in Sarona were spent in practising the men in manœuvring the flat-bottomed boats in a large tank and generally in the perfecting of all plans. The prospect ahead was obviously to the liking of the Colonel, and during these anxious days he wore a broad and contented smile. While in Sarona we received the announcement of the immediate awards granted for gallantry in the Battle of Gaza. These consisted of Military Crosses for David Hannan, M'Combie, Carswell and Souter, and an excellent batch of seven D.C.M.s for N.C.O.s and men of the Battalion.

Weather conditions on the 20th hardly seemed to be favourable, but it was decided not to postpone the venture, and at 6 p.m. the Battalion, along with the other units of the Brigade, marched out of the village into the darkness. My job was as usual with the Administrative Portion, and after the departure of the Battalion I collected the details from each Company at house No. 21, which then became our Headquarters. It was an anxious night, and I spent the greater part of it in the road with John Nicholl listening intently for the dreaded burst of enemy firing, which might mean that the element of surprise was doomed and the whole operation a possible failure. Fortunately, with the exception of our own guns, whose practice during the preceding nights had been to accustom the enemy to constant night firing, no unusual sounds reached us from the direction of the river. Weather conditions proved fickle, for at times heavy rainstorms drenched the troops and the soft ground, while at others dark clouds scudded past and allowed a watery moon to peep out and jeopardize success. Along with returning day the first cheering reports drifted back to us at Sarona, and we anxiously waited orders to push on with the Convoy.

THE LAND OF ORANGE GROVES 133

At 4 o'clock in the afternoon the camels were loaded with water and rations, and we made our way through Summeil to the river. At the village we passed General Hill returning from the captured positions wearing a broad grin of satisfaction. The ground near the river was swampy and the going very difficult, but after considerable delay we crossed the pontoon bridge and turned sharp to the left along a track which boasted a firmer surface. We had no word as to the whereabouts of the Battalion, but M'Alpin, the Camel Officer, who had a happy knack of appearing on such occasions, arrived on his horse, and was able to tell us that we would find it at Muannis, the little village on the high bluff overlooking the river. A little later we were lucky in striking a good firm track, which brought us to the village shortly after 8 p.m.

The village had been badly battered by our guns, but Battalion Headquarters had settled themselves on the ground floor of a good substantial house which was now minus its upper storeys. The two available rooms had been filled with broken bricks, plaster and other debris, and when we arrived Dulieu had just completed a thorough Spring cleaning. The Companies were dotted around in the near vicinity, and we were able to gather some of the details of the previous night's operations.

After leaving Sarona, the troops had passed through Summeil, and reached the river in accordance with schedule. The ground near the point of crossing had become a perfect sea of liquid mud, and unless some means of improvement had been devised it would have been an impossible task for the carrying parties to bring down the pontoons from their hiding-place in an orange grove near by to the place of launching. The inventive mind of the R.E.s came to the rescue. Not far away was a field of sturdy vegetables of the cabbage tribe. These useful denizens of the kitchen garden were uprooted and packed tightly together on the top of the mud. Their stout shaws reduced the slush to a firmer consistency, and the carrying parties passed down to the river on a road of cabbages covered by tarpaulins.

Captain M'Clelland and Steven Bilsland acted as Control Officers during the crossing, and the timetable was so arranged that at no time was there too large a concentration of troops in the immediate neighbourhood of the Bridge. The R.E.s carried out their job with the greatest speed and efficiency, and very soon the flat-bottomed boats and the bridge were in full commission. The 7th H.L.I. of the 157 Brigade crossed the river along with the Battalions of the 156 Brigade. The rôle of this Battalion was to deal from the flank with any attack which might be made upon the other Battalions of the 157 Brigade engaged in crossing the river at the ford. Slight hitches, which could not be foreseen, were quickly overcome, and in a silence which spoke very highly for the discipline of the Brigade, the Battalions were passed over to the other bank. Here the units were re-formed at prearranged points of assembly, and final dispositions made for the attack on the enemy positions.

It was at this point that Captain Humble, while engaged in shepherding toward the rendezvous a

THE LAND OF ORANGE GROVES 135

few of our stragglers who had lost touch in the dark, heard from two voices belonging to men of " Y " Company the classic story of " Yon wee Fella Fergison." The incident recorded by the unknown voices had reference to the person of Captain W. Whigham Ferguson, Commanding " Y " Company, but being recounted in the pithy and picturesque patois of the Army, is not well suited to a literal transcription. One effect of the story was to indicate the affectionate regard in which this officer was held by his men.

For all engaged in the enterprise the time spent in the actual crossing was charged with tension and anxiety. Those feelings were certainly not misplaced, for within five minutes after the last Battalion had moved forward from the north bank, the ground in the immediate vicinity of the bridge was subjected to a heavy outburst of enemy shelling. After our Battalion had reformed, the Companies proceeded to deal in a decisive manner with the enemy posts allotted to them, and it was fully apparent that these attacks came as a complete surprise to the Turkish Garrisons, who either surrendered after a brief resistance or bolted into the darkness. The route to be followed by the Battalion was no easy one. At different points it was necessary to change direction; it was pitch dark, and the ground was of course quite unknown, except in so far as some small localities could be studied by direct observation from the south bank of the Auja or by aeroplane photographs. All movements were made on compass-bearings, and it was a considerable achievement that these were successfully carried through and the final objective hit with absolute accuracy.

Numbers of prisoners were taken, and among the bag was a Turkish Colonel. This officer, with his Headquarters Staff, occupied a house standing at the angle of a wall, and showed considerable disinclination to becoming a Prisoner of War. It required a bombing party, under Anderson of " W " Company, to induce him to change his mind. In addition to a good haul of prisoners, the Battalion captured several machine guns, automatic rifles and innumerable boxes of S.A.A., and a very smart grey Arab horse was added to our stable as a second charger for the Colonel. The operations of the other Battalions of the Brigade likewise met with complete success, and before dawn the remaining enemy forces were pushed well back to a line north of Muannis. The three Battalions of the 157 Brigade had safely crossed the river at the ford, and had cleared the enemy from the region of the sand dunes immediately to the north. The 155 Brigade had been equally successful on the right flank.

Considering the innumerable difficulties and obstacles to be overcome, the discomforts of drenching rain and mud, the absolute necessity for silence and discipline, this night operation by the 52nd (Lowland) Division, involving as it did the forcing of a wide river and the capture of strongly organised and commanding enemy positions, will for long be accounted a military achievement of the first magnitude.

The following is an extract from General Sir

TURKISH TRENCHES CAPTURED ON NORTH BANK OF THE AUJA

THE LAND OF ORANGE GROVES

Edmund Allenby's Despatch, dated 18th Sept., 1918, referring to the forcing of the Auja:

> "The successful crossing of the Nahr El Auja reflects great credit on the 52nd (Lowland) Division. It involved considerable preparation, the details of which were thought out with care and precision. The sodden state of the ground, and, on the night of the crossing, the swollen state of the river, added to the difficulties, yet by dawn the whole of the infantry had crossed. The fact that the enemy were taken by surprise, and that all resistance was overcome with the bayonet without a shot being fired, bear testimony to the discipline of this division. Eleven officers, including two battalion commanders, and 305 other ranks, and ten machine guns were captured in this operation."

The position on the night of the 21st December was roughly as follows: Our troops were now safely established on a line running east and west about a mile north of the river, and in front of our position the enemy, who was now considerably weakened in numbers, had arrested his flight and was occupying a rough line of trenches and rifle pits dug in the sandy soil. At our back flowed the Auja, and it was essential before taking up a permanent defensive line that the bridge-head should be widened until all cross-river traffic should cease to be menaced by Turkish guns and complete freedom of movement could be assured. The time for further action was obviously now, when the enemy was still suffering from the effects of our surprise attack, and during the evening Operation Orders were received for the 22nd.

We spent a fairly comfortable night in the

tumble-down house at Muannis, and at 8 a.m. the Battalion moved out to take part in the general drive forward. The convoy was to remain at Muannis till further orders, and I was able to spend a forenoon of more than ordinary interest. Batteries of Field Artillery clattered past the village, a Field Ambulance arrived and made its arrangements for eventualities, while our old friends the Auckland Mounted Rifles rode in and established their Headquarters in the courtyard near our house. Armed with field glasses, John Nicholl and I made a perilous ascent of a broken staircase which led to the roof of our Headquarters. The roof and upper rooms had been practically demolished, but we were able to find a point on the outer wall from which we could obtain a fine view of the country to the north. The day was then dry and sunny and visibility good.

Very soon the bark of Major Watson's Battery heralded the opening of operations, and we could see the white puffs of shrapnel hanging like bunches of cotton wool above the enemy trenches. Then our lines began to move forward from behind grass-covered hillocks, and the crack of rifle fire swelled the chorus of the guns. As our Artillery fire increased we saw the enemy scurrying out of their trenches and running back over little hill crests to other points of vantage. It was all very spectacular, and from our Observation Post seemed much more like a well-planned Field Day than a full-fledged engagement. Our men went forward rapidly, and when we were no longer able to follow their movements we descended again by the rickety stair, and

THE LAND OF ORANGE GROVES 139

made everything ready to follow on with the convoy as soon as orders might reach us.

While we were engaged in these preparations David Hannan returned to us wearing his arm in a rough sling. He had been winged by a Turkish rifleman, and, leaving his best wishes (and his flask) with M'Combie, who now took over command of "X" Company, had been sent back by the Doctor to find his way to a Field Ambulance.

The Cavalry were still waiting ready if called upon to take part in the pursuit, but for some reason their orders were delayed, and it was midday before they moved out from the village. The message which we expected soon arrived, and at 1 p.m. the Convoy set off to find the Battalion, which was by now several miles out in the blue. The Mounted Orderly who brought the message remained with us as guide, and led us to a point some two miles forward, where we were met by Bruce Allan.

We remained there for some considerable time until all uncertainty as to the position ahead was cleared up, and then pushed on to find the Battalion. The Colonel had sent Darsie back to meet us, so for once we experienced no difficulty or anxiety in tracking down Battalion Headquarters. The day's advance had taken place northward over the southern stretch of the Plain of Sharon, which covers the tract of land between the sea and the foothills. It is a fine rolling country of gentle slopes and shallow valleys with a surface of good sandy turf. We found Battalion Headquarters on a piece of rising ground within a few yards of some rifle pits which a few hours before had been tenanted by the enemy. The evening grew cold and rain threatened, so we lost no time in pitching bivouacs and securing whatever comfort was possible.

The military position appeared to be something like this: Our line now ran east from the sea at Arsuf, past Balutah, until it finally joined with the sector held by the 54th Division just north of Ludd. On this position our troops had halted on a good defensive line, and were now engaged in digging-in about 1200 yards in front of our present Battalion Headquarters. The 157 Brigade was on the left; the 155 Brigade on the right, and in the meantime the 156 Brigade was in support, with two of its Battalions lent to each of the Brigades in the line to help with the work of consolidation. The siting of the Divisional line had been carried out in the afternoon with great rapidity by General Leggett, and it is some tribute to his "eye for ground" that even after the lapse of many weeks the original chain of defences was never altered save in the merest detail.

The weather was now thoroughly broken, and heavy rainstorms, accompanied by half a gale of wind from the south-west, beat down on our little camp. Timber of any sort was difficult to obtain, and it required considerable ingenuity to keep the bivouacs from blowing away. The heavy downpour of the next two days made the transport arrangements from across the Auja a matter of great difficulty, and on the 24th December we realised that Christmas was upon us, and that our

THE LAND OF ORANGE GROVES 141

larder contained nothing but the barest army rations, while the cellar was completely empty, with the exception of a little Sarona wine, which at best was quite incapable of producing anything like an atmosphere of conviviality. We had no tobacco or cigarettes. On the two previous evenings the cook's fire had been washed out when dinner was being prepared, and taking everything into consideration, I did not relish the job of purveying the Christmas dinner, the responsibility for which had been thrust on my unwilling shoulders.

On the night of the 24th John Nicholl and I had managed to strengthen the sides of our bivouac with some planks, and as a special Christmas treat when we went to bed I took off my tunic and boots before getting inside my valise. John was in the throes of a bad bout of neuralgia, which had not been improved by the bitterly cold winds, and was very unhappy. The rain squalls increased in violence, and in the early hours of Christmas morning I was awakened with a strange sense of airlessness about my head, coupled with a very wet and cold feeling about the rest of my body. I soon realised that the bivouac had blown down, that my valise, with any dry garments I possessed, was lying open to the rain, and that the wet folds of the bivouac were lying across my body and face. One of the wooden poles had snapped, but John managed to hold up the other until I fought my way out from under the canvas and pushed my feet into my boots. In the dark and drenching rain we surveyed the ruins of our dwelling, which was now quite beyond repair, and hurriedly rolling up our valises, we carried them down to the Mess dug-out and deposited them on the boxes of S.A.A. which served as the table. Fortunately the canvas roof of the dug-out had withstood the gale, but there was at least half a foot of slimy water on the floor.

Here was a nasty shock to all childhood's dreams of Christmas Eve in the Holy Land. Undoubtedly there should be brilliant moonlight and a calm, clear air, while several shepherds, occasionally bursting forth into a stanza of "Good King Wenceslas" should be at hand watching their large flocks of nice white sheep. And over all imagination should be able to detect the flitting of unseen wings and the lilt of Christmas songs borne through the stillness of the night. It certainly seemed wrong that we should be here sheltering in a water-logged dug-out, while outside the wind howled in derision at the ruins of our bivouac, and violent rain squalls whipped the ground. To make matters worse, John was sitting damp and disconsolate on the top of an ammunition box suffering agonies of neuralgia. Under these circumstances imagination is apt to lose its keenness and humour becomes an elusive comrade.

Conditions throughout Christmas Day remained very unpleasant, and most of the day was spent in trying to arrange for some protection against the weather. Having been betrayed by our bivouac, John and I bent our energies on a dug-out covered over by stout canvas. When it was completed I found that the resourceful Pryer having failed to find anything which he considered really suitable

THE LAND OF ORANGE GROVES 143

for a bed, had laid out my valise on a foundation of fifteen boxes of bombs all ready for use. I thanked him for his Christmas offering.

Our mail was still very far in arrear, and neither letters nor parcels had reached us since leaving Sarona. All the available transport of the army was required to bring rations and supplies from railhead to the troops, and mails, being considered of secondary importance, were left behind. On Christmas morning the Doctor had the luck to receive some tobacco, and we all had a pipe after breakfast. The Battalion Signal Office was busy receiving and sending messages of Christmas greetings.

As the 4th and 7th Royal Scots were now under the orders of the 157 Brigade and the 7th Scottish Rifles and ourselves lent to the 155 Brigade, our own Brigade Staff were temporarily out of a job, and returned in the course of the day to Sarona. Christmas dinner was the best our slender resources would allow, and considering that the cook's fire was again completely washed out at 5 p.m., we did not do badly. During the day I succeeded in acquiring a few additions to the larder, and an issue of rum made an opportune appearance. The menu at dinner consisted of soup, bloaters (tinned), stew of beef and rabbit, with a few potatoes, carrots and cabbage, tinned fruit and toasted cheese on biscuits. On the morning of the 27th the weather cleared, and on that day the Battalion moved to an area about 800 yards further forward, where it would be in more immediate support to the Battalions in the line. From that day until

January 13th the Battalion was constantly employed in sending working parties to help the 155 Brigade with the work of consolidation.

On the night of the 31st December John Nicholl and I retired to "Partionville," our handsome bijou residence, at an early hour. Just before midnight a small avalanche of wild officers descended upon the shack and roused its slumbering inmates in most unseemly manner. A few minutes later we were all grouped round Ollernshaw's dwelling singing that fine old anthem whose verses are designed to prick the uneasy conscience of a Quartermaster. The interrogation in each verse suggested some illicit dealing, as up to the starry heavens rolled in unison the pregnant questions, "Who stole the candles?" or "Who pinched the rum jar?" and always the answer thundered back "Ablooka Alondonuz." Now these were the mystic names with which Ollernshaw had been christened in the days when, with the purest Glasgow accent, we gabbled phrases of Turkish away back at Regent's Park before Gaza. Then having ruined the Colonel's sleep and welcomed the New Year with proper spirit (from Kilmarnock), the night was once more left to the stars, and the sentry pacing up and down by the guard bivouac.

At the beginning of January the first batch of Christmas mail, which had left home at the end of October, arrived. The parcels, after lying for weeks at different points on the lines of Communication, without cover of any sort, and persistently drenched by rain, had eventually been carried back to Kantara by rail and brought to Jaffa by sea

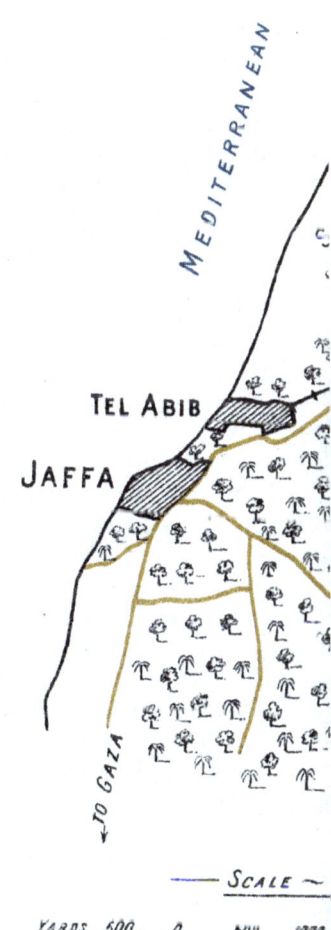

Sketch Showing —
ENVIRONS OF JAFFA
AND RIVER AUJA.

THE LAND OF ORANGE GROVES 145

After the parcels had been distributed there must have been at least a hundred left over, the addresses on which were completely obliterated by the rain, and the contents in many cases reduced to a hopeless condition of mush. By opening these parcels many of the owners were discovered, but there remained a number whose ownership was never established, and these were distributed equally to the Companies. Large quantities of sodden food stuffs and many thousands of rain-ruined cigarettes were relegated to the incinerator.

On 9th January, accompanied by a groom and a pack mule, I rode into Sarona with the object of replenishing our larder and cellar. It was a fine ride as far as the Stone Bridge, but the mud on the other side of the river was quite indescribable, and in spite of the labour of the Pioneer Companies, the country at that part represented the veriest Slough of Despond. I lunched at Brigade Headquarters, and left there the richer by six bottles of whisky, four rum jars of wine and nine pigeons—the latter being the result of a shooting expedition organised for the purpose by the Brigadier. Steven Bilsland rode with me as far as the ford at the mouth of the Auja, where I augmented our supplies by forty fish which some native fishermen had caught in their hand nets. We reached Battalion Headquarters again just after dusk.

On the following afternoon we had a visit from Thomson Brodie, who was engaged in a pilgrimage round the Battalions to secure talent for the Divisional Concert Party, then in process of formation. He eventually stayed the night with us, and

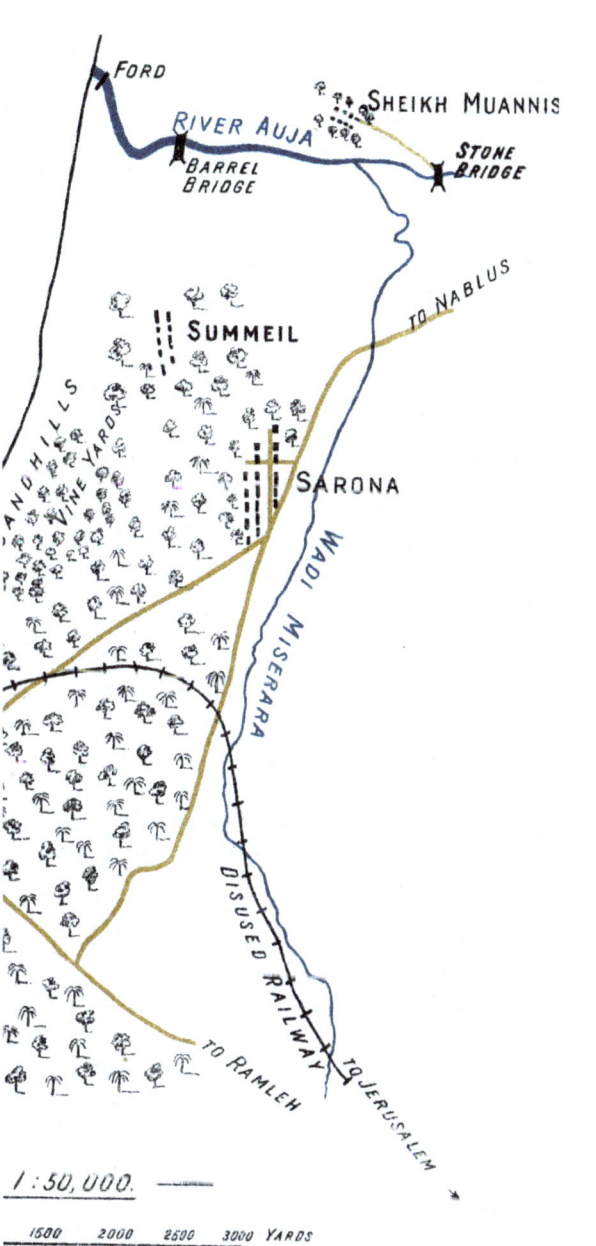

as Dick Coulson also rode over to dinner, we had a cheery evening.

The arrival of Thomson Brodie at the front line a few nights earlier had been quite a notable event. He had set out on horseback in the early afternoon from Divisional Headquarters at Jaffa, and was given a camel on which to carry his kit. After reaching the open country north of the Auja he was overtaken by dusk, and when he reached the neighbourhood of the front line it was quite dark. He must have passed through a gap in the wire between two of our Posts, for the first intimation he received of his whereabouts was when he suddenly found himself surrounded by a number of dark figures with naked bayonets pointing uncomfortably toward his middle. He had fallen into the hands of one of our patrols well out in No Man's Land, and was heading with all speed direct for Turkey.

The work of consolidation on the new line had proceeded rapidly, and we were much cheered by a message from Brigade Headquarters at Sarona, which read something like this, "The Brigadier has won the toss, you will return to Sarona probably on 14th." The question had arisen as to which Brigade would first go into reserve at Sarona, and it had been decided by General Hill that the Brigadiers would settle the point by tossing a coin. This message told us the happy result.

During the past three weeks we had been troubled very little by the enemy, and our Bivouac Area had been lucky in escaping serious damage from the daily shelling.

THE LAND OF ORANGE GROVES 147

On the 13th January I rode into Sarona with a small advance party to have the billets ready for the Battalion on its arrival the following day. Battalion Headquarters was the house immediately next to Brigade Headquarters in the little main street. It was a comfortable dwelling with good accommodation, though as a quiet retreat it possessed the defects of its prominence in being cheek-by-jowl with the Brigade Staff and immediately opposite the Town Major's Office. For to these two houses a constant stream of motor-cars carrying red-hatted officers made their way, and our guard was kept busy running out to accord the necessary honours. For the first time since I had reached the Battalion we were able to have a Battalion Officers' Mess, which was housed in a large marquee pitched on the open ground adjoining Headquarters, and presided over by "Bombs" Westland. Dulieu became head gardener, and the result of his labours was to transform a very bare patch of ground, bordered by an evil-smelling midden, into a real beauty spot with a profusion of plants and flowers. After the Brigade arrived we spent a very cheerful fortnight, with plenty of visitors at our own Mess and a fair amount of dining out. Each evening there was an entertainment at the hall for the men of the Brigade, and there was also an excellent lecture on Jerusalem by Padre Ewing.

Our guests one evening at Mess included the Brigadier, Sayer and a Staff Officer from the XXIst Corps Headquarters. I had received a tip "straight from the stable" that at 10 o'clock that night there would be a practice alarm for the Brigade, with a view to keeping everything keyed up and ready for any emergency. We had a very cheerful meal, and had just embarked on a programme of music when an orderly brought in the fateful message for Sayer, the Brigade Major. The message had, as a matter of fact, been written by Sayer himself some hours earlier, but he played his part well, and having read it with an air of the utmost gravity, handed it to the Brigadier. He likewise carried through the rôle of feigned surprise with great éclat, and in less than a minute all the officers had dispersed to their particular jobs. The XXIst Corps Staff Officer forthwith faded into the night and made off hot-foot for his Headquarters filled with wonderment.

Slacks were hurriedly discarded in favour of breeches and equipment, and everything made ready for a hurried departure in fighting kit to the second line of defence, just north of the Auja. No part of the stage management had been overlooked, and the scenic effect was strengthened when the Brigadier and Sayer were seen emerging from Brigade Headquarters with their loins girt in the breeches of battle. As soon as all Battalions were reported ready to move, the Brigadier told the Commanding Officers that the alarm was merely a practice one.

The evening's entertainment at the Mess had been somewhat ruined, but the officers who returned there were rewarded by hearing Captain Ferguson, accompanied by soft music and labouring under the deepest emotion, deliver himself of his far-famed masterpiece, "The Blue Tail of the Little Yellow Dog." At the conclusion an interesting little ceremony took place when, amid the greatest enthusiasm, Captain Ferguson was invested with the Distinguished Order of the Bowler Hat.

JERUSALEM AND BETHLEHEM

THE RIDE FROM SARONA—SOME SLIGHT IDEA OF THE HILLS
—A HAGGIS IN THE HOLY CITY—A TOUR OF THE HOLY
PLACES—FROM THE VIA DOLOROSA TO THE CHURCH
OF THE SEPULCHRE—BETHLEHEM AND THE CHURCH OF
THE HOLY NATIVITY.

BEFORE going into rest with the Brigade at Sarona, John Nicholl and I had been granted leave for three days by Colonel Findlay and the Brigadier to visit Jerusalem. The Brigadier tried to get us one of the Divisional motor-cars, but as none was available, John and I decided not to miss the opportunity, and set about arranging to carry out the forty-three mile trip on horseback. As this would mean giving us only one clear day in Jerusalem, the Brigadier mentioned that if we overstayed the leave granted by another day no questions would be asked. We left Battalion Headquarters at Sarona at 6.30 a.m. on 24th January. John rode his big Australian; I was on the Padre's horse—selected as being a sturdy animal and a good stayer—and, in addition, we took Copeland, the groom, mounted on "Dick," leading a pack mule carrying rations and forage for the party. It was a lovely morning, but the start was not very auspicious. The load on the pack mule required frequent

JERUSALEM
The City Walls and Mount of Olives from Mount Zion

JERUSALEM AND BETHLEHEM 151

adjustment, and by the time we had passed through the orange groves and reached the Jaffa-Ramleh road, the mule was giving so much trouble that we jettisoned part of the forage and decided to transfer the pack to " Dick " and let the groom ride the mule. The change was certainly not a popular one with "Dick," but after a mile or two he steadied down, and from that time on we had no further trouble.

We reached Ramleh at 9.45 a.m., about an hour behind our schedule, and watered the horses. From Ramleh we made excellent progress, jogging along at a slow trot for a mile or two and then slowing to a walk for a mile, but never stopping. Passing Kubab, we descended the steep hill, and reached Latron at 12 noon. When we left Sarona the plain was covered by a sea of mist, which hid the foothills, but the sun soon brushed the mist aside, until every rock on the hills stood out clear, as though etched against the skyline. The air was crisp and the sun not too hot. We lunched near the roadside about a mile past Latron.

Latron was a supply depôt for the Divisions round about Jerusalem, and was a very busy place. After a halt of less than three-quarters of an hour, we pushed on again. The going across the plains was excellent, for sand rides lie alongside the road, and we were not troubled by the constant strings of motor lorries. About three miles east of Latron the road leaves the plain and quickly loses itself in the hills. The motor convoys from Latron soon became rather a nuisance, but even in the hills we were able at most points to keep off the main road. We had still about seventeen miles to go, nearly all of which had to be done at a walk. We had already acquired a fair experience of these hills, and for mile after mile the path led through narrow passes up over the hill shoulder and down by winding zigzags to the depths of the next valley ; and then the zigzags and corkscrew-turns began again, for another ridge rose in front. Rocks, stony terraces, and occasionally a hardy tree, have for all time been the birthright of these inhospitable hills. Here and there a little grey village, with flat roofs, clings to the hillside, seeking to hide itself in the same drab colourings as the rocks and walls around. We passed Enab (Kirjath-Jearim) at 2.15 p.m.

As we neared the top of each ridge we hoped for some sort of distant view of Jerusalem, but the hills refused to let us go, and we left one ridge behind only to be shut in again by others. Turkish trenches cut in the hillsides, to guard the road and the paths through the valleys, were seen at points of tactical importance. For the last four miles of the journey we left the main road and climbed up over the rough old Jerusalem road. Shortly after leaving Ramleh the Commander-in-Chief passed us in his car going to Jerusalem, and he passed us leaving Jerusalem again just before we reached it. He must have wondered what the little mounted party with the pack animal was.

In the end our hopes of a distant view of Jerusalem came to naught, for turning a corner on the road, we came right face to face with the first houses of the city, only a few hundred yards away. Soon we had passed along the main street, and,

JERUSALEM AND BETHLEHEM 153

leaving the beautiful buildings of the Russian Colony on our left, came to the Hotel Fast at 4.30 p.m. Bourke, the D.A.Q.M.G., on the Governor's Staff, was a good friend, and arranged billets for the horses and groom. The Hotel Fast was able to offer us a good double-room and cooking facilities as long as we supplied the wherewithal to cook. So we were put on the Jerusalem ration strength, and our rations were sent down each day to the hotel. I survived the long ride much better than I expected, and had very little stiffness of which to complain.

We brought with us a parcel which I had received from home a few days before we left Sarona, so we supplemented our rations with some excellent additions, which included a first-rate haggis. We also brought a small supply of whisky, and before leaving Sarona some of the men in the mess—imagining the probable sad state of my health on arrival—had pictured the last precious drops of "Johnnie Walker" being requisitioned to remove the stiffness from my foundations. Bourke dined with us that night, and helped us to deal with the haggis. I fancy the kitchen at the Hotel Fast had never before encountered a haggis.

At 9 a.m. on the following day Bourke supplied us with an excellent guide and passes to enter the walled town. A couple of hundred yards from the hotel is the Jaffa Gate, and just beside it the gap in the city wall made for the entry of the German Emperor in 1898. Just inside the gate is the Citadel, now known as David's tower, and supported by massive walls. An Armenian Church which we entered showed us a very decorative interior, with graceful pillars and a fine sturdy door covered with beaten silver. The guide then led us to Mount Zion, where in one of the buildings, which seem huddled together without any particular plan, we were shown the Chamber of the Last Supper and David's Tomb. Whether or not the positions of these have been accurately verified, the present buildings certainly appeared to be much more modern than the Bible story. And then we went up on to the tower of the German Church near by, which offered a wonderful view of the city and its hills. Down below was the valley of Hinnom, and not far from the outer walls the village of Siloam, resting on the hill slope. I was rather disappointed to find very little evidence of the "shady rills" of which the hymn speaks. There were many churches which the guide was prepared to describe in true guide-book style, but the two points which attracted attention were the Mosque of Omar—which stands in surroundings of great dignity, detached from the welter of bazaars, convents and churches—and the Mount of Olives beyond, standing guard over the city.

The views held us for a long time, and it was here perhaps for the first time that we could realise the vastness of the walls which girdle the town. Then we made our way through narrow bazaars and covered streets, inhabited by a crowd which seemed to differ very little from that to be met in other eastern cities, until an opening brought us out on to the wide Temple area. The Mosque of Omar raises its vast dome in the midst of a huge

JERUSALEM
Mosque of Omar and the Temple Area.

JERUSALEM AND BETHLEHEM 155

paved court, and flights of steps lead down to other broad courtyards flanked by wide cloisters and arcades. A clump of trees lends a softening effect, and there is a certain air of solitude, for the peoples of the streets and bazaars are not here. For simplicity and grandeur the Mosque of Omar, standing on the site of Solomon's Temple, eclipses anything I have seen in Jerusalem. A few yards to the north of the Mosque is a very beautiful kiosk, with delicate pillars and fine mosaics, said to be the site of Solomon's judgment seat. It seemed to be almost feminine in its daintiness. From the Temple area there is a fine view of the Mount of Olives and the Garden of Gethsemane, with the little Russian Church at the corner. The Golden Gate in the north side of the city wall is only a stone's throw away. The gate, which is quite an elaborate structure, is now completely closed up, but we were told of some tradition that Christ at the end of the world will enter Jerusalem by this gate.

Later we crossed the Kidron valley and rode up to the Mount of Olives, stopping for a little while at the Garden of Gethsemane. The Garden is a quiet little walled-in enclosure, with trees and shrubs and little paths, but the wax figures in the glass cases against the walls did not seem to increase its impressiveness. The places were pointed out to us where tradition says that Peter, James and John slept, and where Judas betrayed Jesus with a kiss.

The road to the top of the Mount of Olives is more like the stony bed of a stream than anything else. From the roof of the Church of the Ascension —on the top of the Mount—there is a wonderful panoramic view of the walled city and the surrounding country. Looking toward the city, the Mosque of Omar and its attendant buildings holds pride of place, and although we were able to identify other points, they are for the most part so huddled together as to be difficult to distinguish. There is a good deal of truth in the Psalm which remarks something to the effect that " Jerusalem as a city, is compactly built together." To the east— and apparently only a few miles away—we could catch a glimpse of the Dead Sea and follow the green valley of the Jordan, and on the farther side toward the south rise the deep blue hills of Moab. To the west—some five miles away, but very prominent—is Neby Samwil, of unhappy memory, with its battered Mosque. To the north lie the German buildings, which served as German Headquarters before we captured Jerusalem. And over all was an air clear as crystal and a sky of sapphire blue.

On the way back we sent the horses home, and, entering the city again by the massive Damascus Gate, walked down the Via Dolorosa, which traces Christ's journey with the Cross until it reaches the Church of the Holy Sepulchre. We made a short visit to the Jews' Wailing Place, where the Jews meet and bewail the downfall of Jerusalem ; but since its capture by the British the wailing has become a less popular occupation. Then, as the brain began to reel under the strain of all we had seen and heard, we returned to the hotel, with its

GARDEN OF GETHSEMANE

JERUSALEM AND BETHLEHEM 157

sentry on guard at the door. In the evening we were taken to an excellent pierrot performance in the Empire Theatre, given by the " Barnstormers," the concert party of the 60th Division.

Next day we set out at 9 a.m. for the five mile ride to Bethlehem. The road leads across the Valley of Hinnom and near the railway station, which the Turks partly destroyed before they left Jerusalem. The views from the road to the south and east are beautiful, and it was a most enjoyable ride. Before reaching Bethlehem we passed Rachael's tomb. It is a small domed building quite deserted and in disrepair. Then we went up the hill to the highest part of the town, and obtained the necessary passes at the Governor's Office. It is a pleasant town with many modern buildings and steep paths and narrow streets.

The centre of activity seems to be around the courtyard outside the Church of the Holy Nativity. The church itself is entered by a small, low door in a very high wall ; the reason for the smallness of the door being that experience has taught the Jews to fear trouble from attacks by the Mohammedans. The interior of the church is simple and plain, and has not so many lamps and tinsel as are usual in the other churches. Underneath the choir, steps lead down to the Chapel of the Nativity, where a niche in the rock is shown as the traditional manger where Christ was born. Near the altar there is a large silver star worked into the pavement. After leaving the church, we visited one or two of the shops, and saw the natives working in mother-of-pearl and carving the " Stars of

Bethlehem." The return journey brought us back to Jerusalem by midday.

In the afternoon we made a second visit to the Church of the Holy Sepulchre. I do not think any part of the church—which is really a whole series of churches and chapels—can really be called beautiful, but it is certainly intensely interesting. So great a number of other buildings have been allowed to grow up cheek-by-jowl with the great church that, with the exception of the dome, only a very small part of the exterior of the church itself is visible. This is the façade over the entrance. In decoration it consists of two double arches resting on the top of each other, and before the doorway is a fair-sized stone-flagged court. At first inspection the interior discloses a bewildering welter of religious sects, interests and activities. Almost every article in the building belongs to a different religious body, and should a row of oil lamps—giving forth an evil smell and a bad light—flicker unsteadily before one of the chapels, it is safe to guess that the lamps are the possession in equal proportion of the Armenians, Latins, Greeks and Copts, and that they, and they only, are entitled to burn their lamps at that particular spot. In the centre, under the dome, is the Chapel of the Holy Sepulchre, fashioned in marble. Before the entrance to the chapel hangs the usual row of lamps, flanked by giant candlesticks. The outer chamber of the chapel is very small, and holds the stone which is said to have covered the mouth of the Sepulchre and been rolled away by the angel. Through a low door we came to the Sepulchre

JERUSALEM AND BETHLEHEM

itself, which in size is only about six feet square. On one side is the marble-covered tombstone, and when John and I had entered there was very little room for anyone else. Rows and rows of oil lamps hang from the ceiling, and take away much of the simplicity which might have been expected. The long-robed and bearded attendant, who stood by the end of the tomb and held out a dish for "Backsheesh," hardly seemed to add to the impressiveness of the most sacred spot in the world. Perhaps the other point of greatest interest in the building is Golgotha or Calvary, to reach which we ascended a steep stone staircase at some little distance from the Sepulchre. The chapel here is dimly lit by the familiar strings of lamps, which cast their flickering light on the figure of Christ on the Cross. Near by is a figure of the Virgin, placed in very richly decorated surroundings and adorned with countless pieces of jewellery, offered, we were told, by devout Catholics.

The guide held his long candle down to a point on the ground near the Cross, and showed us a cleft in the rock which is supposed to reach to the centre of the earth. I did not attempt to carry away more than a memory of the countless other chapels and holy places inside this extraordinary building. I was content to take away a general impression of dark, mysterious recesses, flickering lamps and dark-robed priests and attendants moving noiselessly about. As we returned from the chapel on Calvary we met a procession of Roman Catholic priests murmuring Latin prayers and swinging their burning censers to and fro.

Their way led by the final stations of the Cross, the last of which is in the Chapel of the Sepulchre. The atmosphere was laden with incense, mixing with the smells of long tallow candles and ill-trimmed lamps. Anyone who expects to find here a resemblance to the lofty dignity and simplicity of a British Protestant Cathedral may come away unsatisfied with the Church of the Holy Sepulchre.

I have not mentioned the very military appearance of the city. Everywhere round the outskirts of the town were camps and depots, and guards from a Battalion of the London Scottish were mounted at the city gates and at the entrances to all holy places. We saw an Army Service Corps detachment encamped on the Mount of Olives, and the hum of aeroplanes and the sound of the guns reminded us that the British line ran across these forbidding hills, not many miles to the north.

To enjoy Jerusalem to the full it does not really seem necessary to believe that every point shown to-day is the same identical spot which claims connection with the Bible story. And yet, old beliefs and traditions die hard, and these, faithfully handed down from generation to generation by men whose sacred beliefs were their principal stock in trade, while not insuring absolute trustworthiness, have at least a strong claim to probability. For myself, I enjoyed the visit far more than I had ever expected; these old sacred places were seen under the best of circumstances and brilliant weather, and the city—probably owing to the British occupation—was certainly not the dirty, evil-smelling Jerusalem I had been led to expect.

BETHLEHEM
IN THE CHURCH OF THE HOLY NATIVITY

Door in left foreground leads to the niche in the rock said to have been the Manger.

JERUSALEM AND BETHLEHEM

At 6.30 a.m. next morning Copeland brought the horses to the hotel, and ten minutes later we were again on the road. It was a cloudy morning, with a promise of rain. However, it held off for a couple of hours, and we made good progress. About 8.30 we passed through some very heavy showers, and it soon settled down to a thoroughly wet day, with heavy low clouds clinging to the hills. The rides beside the road quickly became so muddy and slippery that we had to keep to the metalled road. At one point in the hills we passed the Donkey Corps, with some 600 diminutive white donkeys, each with its pack saddlery.

We left the hills and came out on to the plain about 10.30, and half an hour later passed Kubab. We intended lunching at Ramleh, but when we arrived there at noon it was raining so heavily that we decided to push on to Sarona. The going was now very heavy, and my horse had developed an occasional stumble, which kept me on the qui vive. However, we held steadily on, and eventually we passed again through the orange groves, and reached Battalion Headquarters at 2.30 p.m. Considering the weather conditions and the state of the roads, forty-three miles in ten minutes less than eight hours is not bad going. It says something for the good condition of the horses, which were in their usual fettle again by the following day—a result entirely due to the care of John Nicholl. Altogether a fine outing and a great relief from Battalion routine!

HERE AND THERE

BACK TO BALUTAH—THE RETURN OF SPRING—AN AIRMAN'S SOUVENIRS—THE BRIGADE MASCOT—UP THE NILE—A WEEK-END WITH THE PTOLEMIES—THE GREAT BARRAGE.

ON returning to Sarona we found that the Brigade was due to relieve the 155 Brigade two days later in the line. Just after noon on the 27th January I set out with an advance party, and crossing the river at the Stone Bridge, struck out for the Battalion Headquarters of the 4th K.O.S.B., whom we were to relieve. The dispositions of the Brigade provided for two Battalions in the front line, with the remaining two in immediate support, and for the first week we were to be in the left sub-section and in support to the 7th Royal Scots. So far as we were concerned, the relief was simple, and by 10 p.m. the Battalion had arrived and begun to settle down. The supplying of night working parties for the front line posts was still the regular routine, and beside these duties, the training of additional Lewis gunners, signallers, etc., was taken in hand. Officers were sent for four-day tours of instruction to different Field Batteries, and Brigade Schools for Bombing and Trench Mortar Work

HERE AND THERE

were organised. In addition to the night working parties, our Battalion supplied patrols, which were sent out each night into "No Man's Land" with varying objects and objectives in view. "Z" Company, who had been assigned the duty of escort to a forward battery of field guns, occupied an area near Balutah and about half a mile distant from the rest of the Battalion.

At this time Dulieu went off on Egyptian leave, and I was kept busy with his work as well as my own. Our quarters were very comfortable, and each of the Battalions in support was issued with about a dozen tents, which were allocated throughout the bivouac area, and thoroughly camouflaged with branches of trees, twigs, rushes, etc. Our canvas-roofed mess dug-out at the top of a little wadi actually boasted a good-going stove, which had been manufatured from a biscuit tin and an old piece of piping.

After being in support for a week, we changed over with the 7th Royal Scots, and took their place in the line. There was no continuous system of trenches, but the posts dotted along the line at short intervals in positions of tactical importance were fortified with earth-works, and the entire line was now closed in with a strong belt of wire. From these posts fine observation was obtained over "No Man's Land" and the Turkish positions which lay along the crest of some rising ground a mile to the north. Just to the right of our sub-section were two plantations, which received constant attention from our patrols.

There were still frequent changes in the weather,

but the intervals between the wet spells gradually bcame longer and a whisper of Spring crept into the air. The countryside became green and fresh, and all around the Battalion area were gentle hill slopes almost hidden beneath a cloak of little blue flowers. Just to the east was the Mukhmar orange grove, and further afield stood out the Turkish village of Tabsor on a rocky eminence formed by a spur of the foothills. Each week or ten days we changed places with our friends the 7th Royal Scots until the inter-relief became almost a matter of routine. With the exception of the daily shelling and the nightly patrols, there was very little in the way of military operations, and any events which happened were for the most part merely of domestic interest. After Dulieu's return from leave he was appointed Assistant Provost Marshal to the 52nd Division, and having been asked by the Colonel to fill the vacancy as Adjutant, I tried to do as much as possible of the Adjutant's work until Dulieu actually left the Battalion.

Quite an event in the comparative calm of these days was the arrival of Captain W. R. Alexander Keeble, who was posted to us from the 2nd Loyal North Lancashires with a view to becoming our Second in Command. He arrived one afternoon at Battalion Headquarters in a motor car piled high with personal luggage and sporting equipment of all kinds. It is a great matter to be prepared for anything, and a pair of skis and a cricket bat seemed to be about the only things lacking to complete his outfit. Some of the Battalions of the 155 Brigade who were then in the section

PYLONS AT TEMPLE OF ISIS, PHILAE

HERE AND THERE

nearest the coast had organised a hunt, and on two occasions Captain Keeble brought back the brush to the Battalion. Sergeant-Major Learmonth, who for years before the War had spent his life among the furry animals in the wilds of Hudson Bay, undertook the curing work, and these trophies of the chase hung from the centre pole of our mess tent.

It was about this time that we heard of a rather remarkable exploit by one of our airmen. He had risen from the Aerodrome at Sarona, and while engaged in a reconnaissance flight some ten miles behind the Turkish line his machine developed engine trouble, which necessitated making an immediate landing. Selecting a quiet spot, where there seemed to be some hope that his descent might pass unnoticed, he landed and quickly set about the necessary repairs. As these were nearing completion he suddenly found that the aeroplane was almost surrounded by Turkish soldiers, and that both he and the machine ran the greatest risk of capture. However, by bringing his Lewis gun into action he kept them at bay, and between the bursts of fire spent anxious and fleeting moments at work on the engine.

Eventually the Turks managed to creep up to close quarters, and just as he had thrown his last ammunition drum in the face of the nearest enemy and all hope of escape seemed to fly away, the engine, apparently for no special reason, burst into spasmodic grunts of life, and the machine moved forward. Fortunately the surface of the ground was fairly smooth, and although he found it impossible to raise the machine to any altitude, the gathering pace sent it bounding forward in a series of long hops. The spectacle of an aeroplane leaping along toward them in great strides was sufficient to scatter the Turks in front, and having shaken off this particular band, the airman reckoned that, once having coaxed the engine again to life, the best hope of returning in safety to our lines was simply to "taxi" home. So with clear eye and steady nerve he set a course where the ground seemed to be fairly even, and, with his machine literally hitting only the high places, made good progress.

When approaching the Turkish line he found himself unexpectedly passing through a scattered encampment, and in a flash he realised that he was among the officers' lines. A string, with a number of pieces of cloth suspended therefrom, was stretched across his path, and although the propellor escaped being fouled, the string could not be altogether cleared, and was carried away hitched round the tail of the machine. The Turks were so surprised at the uncanny sight of an aeroplane stalking through their camp that they did not open fire until the opportunity along with the machine had fled. With the hop of a giant kangaroo the airman succeeded in clearing the Turkish trenches and wire, and, speeding across "No Man's Land," finished up with another jump, which brought him well behind our own lines at Balutah and into safety. Not only had he succeeded in reaching his haven under very unusual circumstances, but he had brought back with him some unique souvenirs

HERE AND THERE

of the escapade. It had been washing day in the Turkish camp, and the string and pieces of cloth, which were now firmly secured to the tail of his machine were nothing but the clothes rope with pendent shirts and other intimate garments belonging to the Turkish officers.

While we were at Balutah, Sayer left for home to attend a Staff Officers' Course, and I dined at Brigade Headquarters on the night before his departure. The Brigade Mess was housed in a snug little hut, and its furnishings included an excellent stove imported from Sarona. From the ceiling of the hut was suspended the Brigade mascot and emblem of a sudden return to civilian pursuits in the shape of a silk top hat, which in times of peace had no doubt crowned the august head of the Mayor of Sarona. It was hanging there when the Corps Commander visited Brigade Headquarters, but although he cast an apprehensive glance in its direction, he made no comment.

During these weeks my name had been creeping up on the roster for Egyptian leave, and on 10th March John Nicholl and I left railhead at Ludd *en route* for Cairo.

Arrangements for officers going on leave were well organised. When our application was approved by the Divisional General, sleeping berths were at the same time reserved in the Leave Special which started from railhead each evening.

On the previous afternoon we rode into Sarona, and dined with Allan Rogers, who had become Divisional Requisitioning Officer. We slept at the dismal and inhospitable Details Camp, and on the forenoon of the 10th rode over to Ludd. Pryer and Hall preceded us with the baggage on a limber. The Leave Special brought us to Kantara East about 6 a.m. on the 11th, and motor lorries awaited the train to transport officers and baggage across the Canal to Kantara West. The train for Cairo did not leave till 10 a.m., and the intervening hours were occupied with the morning toilet and an excellent breakfast in the Rest Hut near the station, presided over by Mrs. Chisholm. By 2 p.m. we were in the Continental Hotel, Cairo, and surrounded by every luxury.

We decided to push on as soon as possible to Assouan, so after a breezy dinner at Shepherd's Grill with Ramage of the 4th Royal Scots, followed on the 12th by a luncheon party with Dai Carson and an appearance at one of Lady Allenby's dances, we started off at 8 p.m. in a sleeper for Assouan. When we reached Luxor we met Dr. Sloan, by chance, on the platform, and he joined us in the comfortable but very dusty compartment of the little train which runs along the banks of the Nile to Upper Egypt. The thermometer rose steadily as we made our way south, and at 4.30 p.m., when we ran into the station at Assouan, it was easy to realise that we had journeyed nearly a thousand miles from our starting-point at Ludd. At Assouan the river widens out, and dotted here and there are countless islands. Just at sunset we walked up to some beautiful gardens laid out on a promontory overlooking the river and watched the ever-changing views. The little islands, with their shock-headed palms and fringes of sandy beach,

THE GREAT BARRAGE NEAR ASSOUAN

HERE AND THERE

were a blaze of greenery, while the brightly-painted Nile boats, with their long tipsy-looking masts, nodded sleepily to the current. The colourings were superb, and the flowers in the gardens filled the air with their fragrance.

On the following day we became trippers of the most approved pattern, and spent a wonderfully interesting day of sight-seeing. This included an early start, when we rode on donkeys across a short stretch of the Nubian desert to Shellal. Here we embarked on a small sailing boat, and in an hour's time had reached Philae. All that can now be seen of the Island is the roof of the Temple of Isis with its two massive Pylons, and the upper portion of a kiosk, the roof of which is supported by pillars with finely-carved capitals, against which the water now laps. We walked over the roof of the temple, marvelled at the carvings, and looked down into chambers completely submerged under the dark waters. It was difficult to realise that these were the waters of a mere river, for the appearance around was all of a vast inland sea. And when the guide, who made use of the carvings as a school blackboard, had taken us on a quick tour through the ancient dynasties, had introduced us to each of the Ptolemies in turn, and then started down the list of Pharaohs, we gasped for breath and made a hurried escape in the boat.

From the Ancient we proceeded to the Modern, and came to a little landing-stage at one end of the Great Barrage. I was certainly astonished at the immensity of this vast engineering achievement, for the huge belt of solid masonry, which holds in check these surging currents and carries the machinery controlling the sluices by which the waters of the lower Nile are regulated, is over a mile in length. Sitting on a trolley, which was pushed from behind by two natives, we crossed to the Government Offices, and on the way we got off to watch the water rushing forth from a series of open sluices. Huge volumes shot forth in great solid curving masses, sending clouds of spray high into the air, and driving on, foamed and curled among the rocks and islets of the cataract below.

We lunched at the offices, where a Company of a Native Regiment was on guard, with their machine guns posted on the roofs of the buildings. We were told that the Desert folk had reported seeing a Zeppelin not many miles away, but little belief was then attached to their tale. It would seem, however, from later official German accounts of the voyages of their Zeppelins that this was no mere yarn of the imagination, and that this particular Zeppelin was the German airship which sailed from its eyrie in the Balkans in the hopes of carrying medical supplies to the German forces in East Africa.

And then we walked down past the lock gates in the canal at the west side of the barrage, where little brown urchins dive from dizzy heights for coins into the water below, and found the boat which was to carry us back to Assouan. It was quite an exciting little trip, shooting the rapids between the islands with the waters swirling and foaming alongside, and with a gentle breeze on the big sail we soon passed under the rocky bluff which looks

HERE AND THERE

across to the Island of Elephantina, and tied up under the trees which fringe the road at Assouan.

Later we rode on donkeys to the Camp of the Bisharin, and saw the real original "Fuzzy Wuzzies" in their miserable dirty native tents. The Stone Quarries behind the town are interesting, and the notches are still visible where in ancient days the wooden wedges swelled with water and forced out the huge blocks of granite, which were carried on floats down the Nile to Luxor and used in the construction of the Temples. Later we visited the Island of Elephantina, but by this time my enthusiasm as a tripper had become strained, and its ruins and antiquity left me rather cold.

On the return trip to Cairo, we broke the journey for four hours at Luxor, and made a hurried visit to Karnak. We wandered along the Avenue, lined on either side by rows of Sphinxes, which in the old days led down to the banks of the Nile, and passed through the vast halls and colonnades, with their forests of huge pillars. An hour's visit to the Great Temple of Ammon at Karnak may provide a lasting memory of colossal size, great ungainly statues, ancient stone carvings, a wealth of smaller temples, a myriad inscriptions and finely proportioned obelisks, but the historical associations binding the whole together are a pure bewilderment. And so it was at the Temple of Luxor, which we visited when the afternoon heat yielded to an evening air from across the river. However, during the past two days we had achieved at least a bowing acquaintance with several

Rameses and one or two Ptolemies, and were on terms of comparative intimacy with such things as Pylons, Hypostyle Halls, Cartouches, etc., which are lavishly scattered throughout the vocabulary of the Temple Guides.

Next morning found us suffering slightly from mental indigestion caused by an overdose of Antiquity, but back in Cairo among the comforts of the Continental Hotel. On the evening of the 20th March we recrossed the canal at Kantara, and were once more swallowed up in the iron gullet of the Military Machine.

IN THE TEMPLE OF AMMON, KARNAK, LUXOR

THERE'S A RUMOUR

There's a rumour come up from the Transport lines ;
  A rumour that's quite untrue ;
But as well as on Water and Rations
  We thrive on the rumours too.

It's a beautiful, fanciful story
  Of a gun of gigantic size,
That is lying at rest in its deep-dug nest
  By the tree on the sandy rise.

The Division is off to Archangel—
  To the frosts and the ice-covered seas ;
There's a talk of an issue of snow-boots,
  And of hot-water bottles and skis.

Or it may be that Peace is concluded,
  Or a month's home leave for all :
The selection is vast, and its speed will be fast
  If the yarn be sufficiently tall.

Embroider them well in the telling—
  They die if they're simply ignored ;
So show no surprise though you know they are lies,
  But be glad of the smile they afford.

WESTWARD HO !

WESTWARD HO!

RUMOURS—FAREWELL TO PALESTINE—H.M.T. "CANBERRA"
—FINAL RECONNAISSANCES AT ALEXANDRIA—THE
DIVISION AT SEA.

We reached Ludd on the morning of 21st March, and finding our horses waiting for us, we set out after breakfast, and reached Sarona at midday. The Brigade had come in from the line a few days previously, and the Battalion was settled down in very comfortable quarters. I shared a room with Dulieu in the Officers' Mess House.

Colonel Findlay had left for Cairo the previous day on leave, and Alexander-Keeble was temporarily in command. In the evening two days later I rode into Jaffa with John Nicholl to see a performance of "The Thistletops," who were playing to crowded houses in the Jaffa Theatre. The Divisional Troup was the child of Major-General John Hill; was nursed into robust life by Thomson Brodie, and the party now produced a first-class pierrot entertainment. War provides many surprises, but I certainly never expected to find Thomson Brodie lurking behind the stage door of a Jaffa theatre clad in the raiment of a pierrot, with his face disguised beneath a thick layer of paints and cosmetics.

During the following days the suggestion of a sudden move began to be whispered with some air of conviction, and the receipt of a warning order instructing units to be prepared to take the road at shortest notice produced one of the finest crops of rumours. Excellent reasons were adduced why the Division should, or should not, proceed to each particular theatre of War, ranging from India to East Africa or Archangel, and although the answer to the riddle did not seem to demand a great strain on the imagination, our destination was wrapped in profound official secrecy. The reasons underlying every Order were scrutinised in piercing fashion and made to dovetail into every conceivable theory. They were certainly days of much suppressed excitement.

One evening we had a very successful Mess Dinner, to which a number of guests were invited. It was a very cheerful gathering, the only unfortunate and unusual incident about it being that one of the guests broke his ankle. The Army Form which was subsequently filled up in our Orderly Room with a short description of the circumstances of the accident contained more underlying humour than is usually to be found on the buff-coloured face of an official document.

On the 27th March we received orders to proceed on the following night to a bivouac area at Surafend, near Ramleh, and very comprehensive arrangements were made so that all kit, baggage and gear of every description, which was now considerably in excess of the amount for which transport was nominally provided, should accompany the Battalion.

On 28th March Dulieu left the Battalion to take up his duties as Divisional A.P.M. The Battalion owed him a big debt of gratitude, and personally I was very sorry when he rode away, for we had worked together for many months, and under all sorts of circumstances. On the same night the Brigade marched out from Sarona, and as we took our place in the column and passed down through the groves we realised with a tinge of regret that we were not likely to return again to the little village. It was quite dark when we reached Surafend, but by midnight we were safely installed in our new bivouac area. During the next few days our other Brigades were relieved in the line by the 7th (Indian) Division, and the 52nd Division concentrated at Surafend.

Our own Brigade took the opportunity to complete the Sports which had been interrupted by our hasty departure from Sarona, and quantities of stores which would not accompany us further were returned to Ordnance. When the gas respirators which a few weeks previously had been handed in, were again drawn and issued to the men, the sign posts on our road seemed to point with conviction towards the West. Scott was sent off hurriedly to Cairo and Alexandria to square up Mess accounts or transact private business for the officers. It was a sad day when our transport left the Battalion. Many of us said good-bye to a tried and trusty friend among the horses, while John Nicholl seemed suddenly to have been bereft of his entire family, and moved about with an air of complete desolation. Meantime the Colonel had returned from leave, and Alexander-Keeble, who was to remain behind in Palestine, was transferred to another Division, and rode away into the haze of war, which covers the tracks of many old comrades.

On the 1st April Captain G. R. V. Hume Gore, M.C., of the Gordon Highlanders, was attached to us, and took up the duties of Second in Command. The 156 Brigade was the first to move down the line, and shortly after midday on 3rd April the Battalion marched off from Surafend for the entraining station at Ludd. The Colonel and I had borrowed two horses from the officers of a Camel Company, and their syces accompanied us to take them back from the station. My own beast was a quiet animal, but the Colonel had a young horse with evil manners. All went quietly till we came out on to the main road, but there the Colonel's animal jibbed and shied at each of the many motor cars, ambulances or lorries which passed the column. There were very deep and broad drainage trenches on each side of the road, and less space was therefore available for the management of an unruly horse. As the Colonel was in process of dismounting the beast lunged forward, with the result that the Colonel fell heavily on his head on the hard road. He was quite unconscious when we picked him up and carried him to the roadside, and when the Doctor had taken him in charge, I reported to Hume Gore, and told him the Command now devolved on him.

WESTWARD HO! 179

Meantime the Battalion had moved on, and we were able to stop a motor ambulance, which took Colonel Findlay to the hospital, whose tents lay among the trees near Ludd Station. I reached the entraining point myself in another motor before the Battalion arrived, and found that already John Nicholl and Ollernshaw had completed the loading of the baggage, while Innes had arranged the other details of entrainment. Before leaving, I was able to make a hurried visit to the hospital and learn the Colonel's condition, and when the train steamed out at 6 p.m. we were waved off by Dulieu, who had come down to say au revoir, all tabbed and hatted in red. He certainly got a rousing cheer from the men of the Battalion.

We arrived at Kantara at 8 a.m. on the 4th, and spent the day at one of the Infantry Base Depots. When we were here I heard this tale. One of the Battalion officers some time before had been at Kantara, in which at that period nearly all the troops happened to be English. When walking one day along the hard-baked road in the glare of the sun he was saluted by a passing private. Something in the figure of this particular private seemed familiar, and the officer recognised him as Private Mutchkin—an erstwhile member of his Company who had eventually left the Battalion and drifted to Kantara on some detached duty. Incidentally the officer knew him as a lovable rascal, a first-rate man in action, and possessed of a sense of smell capable of detecting the presence of a bottle of beer at the other side of the Sahara. The officer stopped, and with the interest of old comradeship asked him how he was getting on. The conversation was brief, but pregnant with meaning.

Officer: "Well, Mutchkin, glad to see you. How are you getting on?"

Private M. (taking upon himself an unusual air of dejection, but confident of receiving sympathy from an old friend): "Well, Sir, to tell ye the truth, I've been in trouble."

Officer (knowing by experience the probable nature of said trouble): "Why, what's gone wrong?"

Private M. (confidentially, but in measured tones of complete contempt): "Well, ye see, Sir, it's like this: thae English folk don't understand aboot drink."

No further explanation was necessary.

During these days we were constantly occupied with arrangements connected with the move, and on the 4th we increased the strength of the Battalion by six new officers, and all the details of grooms, batmen, storekeepers, etc., who had hived off to various jobs during the progress of the unit through Egypt and Palestine, and had now been collected together to accompany us to France. Dai Carson dined with us at night, and by 2 a.m. on the morning of the 5th April we had entrained from the siding at Kantara East and set out for Alexandria. Eight hours later we reached our destination and detrained at Gabarri, the station beside the Docks.

Our ship, H.M.T. "Canberra," was tied up to the quay immediately opposite our train, and embarkation proceeded forthwith. By noon the

WESTWARD HO!

ship's company, which consisted of the 8th Scottish Rifles, 156 Machine Gun Company and Trench Mortar Battery, a part of the 1st Lowland Field Ambulance and a few details, was all on board. Hume Gore was appointed O.C. Troops, and I again drew the job of Ship's Adjutant.

Having finished his work in Cairo and Alexandria, Scott had rejoined us, and had brought for me a box which, since my arrival in Egypt, had been deposited with Cox & Co. In this I had kept copies of all the Ship's Orders I had written on the "Transylvania," and these proved a great help. With a ship's company composed entirely of completely organised units, the work of Ship's Adjutant was simple in comparison to my previous experience. The "Canberra" was a ship of some 7000 tons, and in peaceful days had been employed on the Australian Coastal Service. Her quarters were comfortable, and the Skipper and officers most friendly and helpful. The other three Battalions of the Brigade were on the "Leasowe Castle," a Union Castle boat of about 15,000 tons.

On the night of the 5th a party of men from the Brigade became filled with a desire to carry out a final reconnaissance of the town, and succeeding with no little skill in passing the sentries and dock picquets, marched as a formed body into Alexandria. Here the party broke up, and later on the majority, having become a very cheerful and happy band of warriors, failed to meet with the complete approval of the Military Police, and were given a night's lodging in the Main Guard. Which exploit leads to a yarn regarding Colonel

W. C. Peebles, D.S.O., of the 7th Royal Scots. He and Colonel A. M. Mitchell of the 4th Royal Scots were hurriedly invited by the G.O.C. Alexandria District, who, I am afraid, was so inhospitable as to regard our Division as being somewhat in the nature of unwelcome guests, to visit the inmates of the Main Guard. When the door was opened and Colonel Peebles, erect of stature and stern of countenance, surveyed the inmates, a voice breaking the silence and speaking in accents curiously reminiscent of the Haymarket was heard to murmur: "Oh Lord, they've brought the Colonel in too."

On the afternoon of the 6th, the "Canberra" pulled out to the outer harbour, and there we awaited the day when the entire Division would be ready to sail. To keep the men employed and interested we organised a series of team races in the ship's boats and a very successful boxing tournament. Concerts were also arranged, and on one day a lighter, with two barges in tow, came alongside and took off the men in batches to bathe at the breakwater.

On the 9th I dined ashore at the "Majestic" with Hume Gore, John Nicholl, Steven Bilsland, and Major Archer, the A.P.M. of Alexandria. The entire dining-room was filled by a cheerful family party from the Division, but our guest, the A.P.M., seemed somewhat distraught and overburdened by the responsibilities of his official position, and I doubt if he thoroughly enjoyed his meal.

On the following day I attended a conference of all

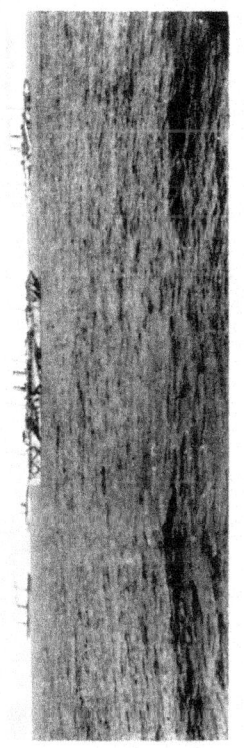

"OMRAH," "INDARRA," "LEASOWE CASTLE," "KAISER-I-HIND"
Convoy carrying the 52nd (Lowland Division) to France, taken from "Canberra"

WESTWARD HO! 183

Officers Commanding Troops on the Transports and Ships Adjutants, which was held at the Embarkation Headquarters. Here final and confidential instructions for the voyage were given, and the secret code words were verbally communicated. After the conference one of the Embarkation Officers took Hume Gore and myself in his launch to the hospital at Ras-el-Tin to see the Colonel, who had arrived there a day or two previously from Ludd. The hospital stands on a spit of land near the end of the breakwater, and hard by is the Sultan's Summer Palace of Ras-el-Tin. The Colonel looked a very different man from the one I had seen on the roadside at Ludd. He was bitterly disappointed at the prospect of the Division sailing away without him, and he suggested that I should arrange something which sounded very much in the nature of a kidnapping expedition with a view toward smuggling him aboard the "Canberra." After leaving him, we had tea at the Yacht Club, and then returned to our ship.

By this time the other two Brigades had embarked, and the Convoy being now ready to sail, we were told that the voyage would start on the 11th April. On each of the two previous days a boat had been sunk by enemy submarines not far from the entrance to the harbour, and just before our Convoy was due to sail, a number of depth charges were dropped as a measure of precaution by Destroyers along the channel which we would take. There was apparently no evidence that " U " boats were in the vicinity, and at 2 p.m. the ships of the Convoy filed slowly out of the harbour. It was a lovely day of bright sunshine and light airs, and it was a fine sight to see the big Transports follow each other in line-ahead.

The Convoy which carried the 52nd Division consisted of seven boats—" Canberra," " Leasowe Castle," " Omrah," " Malwa," " Indarra," " Kaiser-i-hind " and " Caledonia," while our escort was composed of six Japanese Destroyers and a British Sloop. " Omrah " being the slowest of the Convoy, was flagship, and all changes of course were directed from her bridge. One of the chief danger spots for submarines was just outside the harbour, and during the first few miles, while we moved along the line of buoys which mark the channel, the Destroyers scurried about, racing forward and doubling back in their white wakes like hounds at fault. Then in turn the pilots were dropped, and the Convoy swung to the west in prearranged formation. " Canberra " was on the left flank, and a little Japanese Destroyer raced up and took its place as flank guard on our port bow. Soon the low coastline dropped beneath the horizon as the Magnet of War drew the Lowland Division to fresh fields in the West. The Convoy was an imposing and stately affair, with four ships in the first line and three behind, all being decked out in a perfect intoxication of camouflage.

Now and then a flutter of bunting from "Omrah's" bridge signalled a change of course, and the whole fleet would wheel round with wonderful precision. All day and night the little Jap Destroyers clung like limpets to our sides, and very comforting they were. Occasionally one

WESTWARD HO!

would dart ahead or out to the side and lay a zig-zag pattern of white foam on the blue sea, then having apparently expended its surplus energy, would quietly return to its appointed station.

Life on board the " Canberra " was very pleasant, as we had good deck accommodation, and the men's quarters were reasonably comfortable and the messing good. During the afternoons and evenings the men lay about the decks, while here and there a loud voice would chant long series of numbers, interspersed with an occasional shout of " Tap o' the Hoose." As a form of entertainment the game of " House " was an easy winner. The Machine Gun Company manned six of their guns, which at different points were lashed to the deck rails and ready for immediate action, while the Trench Mortar Battery supplied the ammunition carrying parties, which were constantly on duty with the two naval ratings at the ship's gun. Colonel Leitch, with the men of his Ambulance, took professional pride in all sanitary arrangements, while the remaining guards and duties fell to the Battalion. Before leaving Alexandria harbour the day's programme had already become a matter of routine, which continued successfully throughout the voyage. Our route lay to the south of Malta, but with the exception of a short glimpse of blue hills on the African coast, we sighted no land.

The Chief Officer was an excellent man of large and cheerful presence, and with countless weird experiences to his credit. His cabin underneath the upper bridge became a delightful retreat, where, along with other forms of hospitality, we were regaled with many strange tales of the seas. From him I occasionally heard whispers from the wireless-room of danger spots looming ahead or safely passed, but fortunately no submarine showed itself.

And so the days slipped past, until early on the morning of the 17th April we found ourselves face to face with the coast of France, and moving again in line-ahead toward the entrance gate of the boom defences at Marseilles. The final order issued on board ran as follows :

> The O.C. Troops, in the name of all ranks on board, thanks the Commander, Officers and Crew for a safe and comfortable voyage, and hopes that " Good Luck " may accompany all voyages of H.M.T. " Canberra."

Grey skies looked down on the Convoy as we arrived, and when we moved slowly through the entrance to the harbour, we finally passed out of the Chapter of War which deals with the Armies of the East and entered upon the ultimate phase of the Great Adventure.

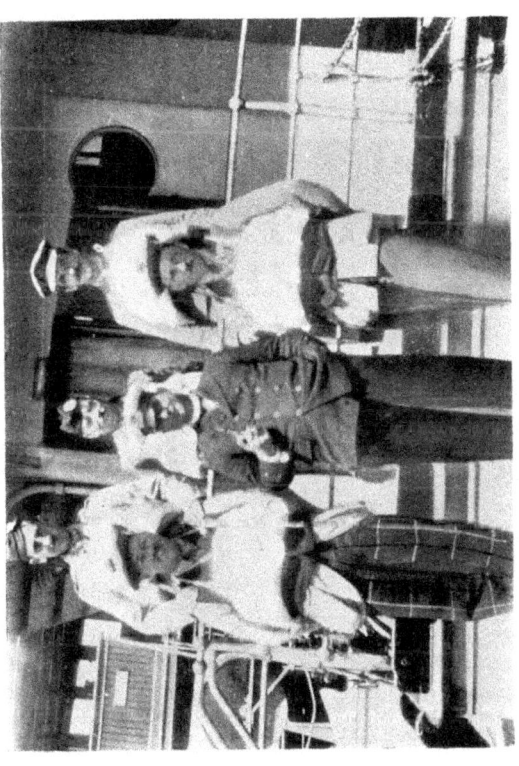

H.M.T. "CANBERRA," THE STAFF

Lieut. J. M. Nicholl Hon.-Lieut. J. Ollernshaw Lieut.-Col. J. A. Leitch, D.S.O., R.A.M.C.
Capt. E. R. Boyd Chief Officer Major G. R. V. Hume-Gore, M.C.

FRANCE

FROM MARSEILLES TO THE BACKMOST AREA—LESSONS IN FRIGHTFULNESS—AT VIMY RIDGE—AU REVOIR TO THE 52ND DIVISION—P.P.C. LETTERS—HOME LEAVE—TO FLANDERS AND THE 34TH DIVISION—TO ANOTHER FRONT BY TRAIN, BUS, AND MARCH ROUTE—WITH THE FRENCH AND AMERICANS—THROUGH THE FORESTS—ON THE FRINGE OF BATTLE—IN THE CARE OF THE FRENCH MEDICAL SERVICES—EXPLOITS WITH A FOREIGN TONGUE—A BRITISH RED CROSS HOSPITAL IN FRANCE—HOME.

By 2 p.m. on the 17th April the disembarkation of the Battalion was complete, and we marched off to Camp Fournier, which was the nearest camp to the town. Our first experience of Staff work in France was rather impressive, for no sooner had our ship been tied up to the dock than several sacks of home mail were brought on board, and we had the unusual satisfaction of reading letters less than a week old. The entrainment of the Division had already begun, but the military trains only ran at three-hour intervals, and our own particular Special was not due to leave till 1.30 p.m. on the following day. I dined at night with Hume Gore at the "Bristol," where we found that the toll of

War since 1917 had made deep inroads into the menu, and simple sugarless fare was now the order of the day.

At noon on the 18th we entrained at Point 1, and were waved off to our unknown destination by John Tulloch, whose responsibilities included the entrainment of the entire Division. I shared a compartment with Hume Gore, and as we passed along the cliffs we had our last view of the Mediterranean, which lapped against the rocks far below. The chief feature of our journey north was the intense cold, and my eiderdown quilt was a constant, close and warm friend. Not only had we come direct from a very hot climate, but on arrival in France we had the evil fortune to strike a spell of keen frost, which overnight transformed the washing water in our canvas buckets into solid ice. We now had our first opportunity to learn the details of the German drive which the Allies had stemmed at the beginning of the month, and we realised that it would not likely be long before we took our place in the line.

Hume Gore had his own ideas as to the type of rations suitable to a three days' journey, but these, though dainty in conception, were in effect somewhat messy. However, armed with a superannuated tin-opener, he seemed thoroughly to enjoy constant hand-to-hand encounters with tins of Pâté de Foie Gras, Sardines, Honey, Preserved Fruit, etc., and I was perfectly content to watch and applaud his efforts and incidentally to share in the fruits of his victories. During each day there was at least one long "Halte du Repas," when hot tea was issued to the men, and we were able to find an opportunity for a shave, wash, and occasionally an omelette in a handy café.

The men certainly made light of the cold, but must have suffered greatly, for though the military idea of the number of passengers required to fill a compartment is likely to produce a certain atmosphere of warmth, the men had not yet received an issue of underclothing. On the forenoon of the 20th we skirted the suburbs of Paris, and entered a country of endless camps, hutments and dumps. Frequently we passed crowded trains of French soldiers, from whom we received a rousing welcome to the Armies of France.

At 6 a.m. on the 21st we reached our immediate destination, which was Noyelles—a town not far from Abbeville, at the mouth of the Somme—and there we detrained and breakfasted at a Rest Camp. In the forenoon we proceeded by march route to Le Butte des Crocs, a little hamlet which lay about eight miles distant from Noyelles. We lunched by the roadside, and I called with Hume Gore at Brigade Headquarters, which were already established at a village near by. At 2.30 p.m. we came to our journey's end, and reached the little village green, where we found Innes and the Advance Party. Innes, as Assistant Adjutant, had gone ahead with the baggage, and had the billeting arrangements completed when we arrived. Battalion Headquarters settled itself in a house near the green, while "W," "X," and "Z" Companies were each allotted a large farm with roomy barns. "Y" Company was lucky in finding an excellent billet about two miles from Battalion Headquarters. It was a very large and tidy farm owned by a gentleman farmer, and in view of their surroundings and comfort, the members of "Y" Company wore a slightly superior air.

At Le Butte des Crocs we were many miles from the battle zone, and here we settled down to a few days of exercise and training after our long journey. Ollernshaw secured supplies of warm clothing for the men, and at this time the frosty weather fortunately came to an end. Home mails reached us daily, and this fact alone seemed to reconcile us to France. On arrival we came under the orders of the Reserve Army, and for all we ever knew the 52nd Division may actually have comprised that entire force. Among the excellent things which hold a place in my memory is the rum punch which was manufactured by the Lady of the Estaminet which served as a billet for John Miller, Carswell and the Doctor.

While at Le Butte des Crocs we were again provided with transport, and John Nicholl, who during the move from Palestine had acted as Baggage Officer, came into his own once more. But our Transport Establishment now made a tame show bereft of our old friends the camels and little white donkeys, and we lost much of the interesting appearance of a travelling circus.

The 25th April found us in the thick of packing, for we were due to leave Rue by train at 8.30 p.m. on the next stage of our wanderings. The march to the station was only some three miles, and there we found Steven Bilsland deep in entraining states,

FRANCE

but still in full possession of a cheerful outlook on life. Our route during the night took us much nearer the line, and the guns considerably disturbed our slumbers.

At eight o'clock in the morning we detrained at Wizerne, and we had expected to be billeted in a particular village near at hand. However, at the last moment all plans were changed, and after breakfasting in a field beside the station, we set out on a ten mile march in another direction, which brought us in the afternoon to the town of Mametz. Innes had gone on ahead with a small party on bicycles, and when we found him in the main street of Mametz about 2 p.m. he was still battling gallantly with the difficult job of trying to billet the Battalion in a district of the town where practically no billets existed. It appeared that the Town Major had been warned that a Brigade was coming in, but the Brigade he expected to arrive was one composed of three attenuated Battalions of 300 men each. When, instead of this, a Brigade of four Battalions, each with some 800 men, marched into the town the question of suitable accommodation became a distinct problem, and the Town Major retired in hopeless despair to his office.

Before leaving Le Butte des Crocs, a French Sergeant of the Interpreter's Corps had been posted to our Battalion. He was a quaint little fellow, with legs so short that they could not fit the regulation frame of army bicycle. As he was really only of use for billeting work, and as billeting parties almost invariably were called upon to use bicycles, his usefulness became strictly limited, and all my efforts toward coaxing him to become an enthusiastic cyclist were of no avail. He had one characteristic in common with all good soldiers, for he always succeeded in finding a first-rate billet for himself. And when circumstances led the Battalion to unpleasant localities his duties always seemed to take him elsewhere.

We found that the previous tenants of our quarters at Mametz had been a Portuguese Regiment, and for some reason the townsfolk did not appear to be enthusiastic over subsequent arrivals. However, by 7 p.m. we had found cover for all the men, and were tackling the question of accommodation for the officers when the Brigadier met us and asked Hume Gore and myself to dine at Brigade Headquarters. Eventually temporary quarters in houses or barns were found for all the officers, and being then in an advanced stage of starvation, I set out for the Brigade Mess.

At this time the Brigade Staff presented quite an imposing array, for along with the Brigadier it consisted of Metcalfe, who had taken Sayer's place as Brigade Major, Bruce Allan, Steven Bilsland, M'Clelland, Stanley Smith, a Gas Officer, and a French Officer of the Interpreters' Corps. Dinner was already in progress when I arrived, and before I had actually sat down a cork popped at right angles to my ear, and a complete bottle of beautiful bubbling liquid was placed on the table beside me. In the midst of the great events of war it is curious how many of the best remembered incidents centre round such apparently trivial affairs as a drink provided on a sweltering day by some kind

FRANCE

Samaritan, a pull at a flask amid the cold and wet of the hills, some well-stewed tea from a mess-tin lid on a filthy night in the trenches, or a good dinner and a bottle of champagne at a time when the body is weary and meals uncertain.

On the 27th April we eased the pressure at Mametz by moving Battalion Headquarters to the little village of Glomenghen, about a mile away, and there we remained until 8th May. The farmhouse in which we lived was the typical variety laid out on a square plan, with the buildings all facing toward a large manure heap in the middle. The womenfolk were good kindly souls, who brewed excellent coffee and heated water for our baths. Here we lived well within the sound of the guns, and in the evenings the eastern sky was alive with flash and flame.

The days were strenuous, for from morning to night we were coached and tutored in the niceties of the Game as played in France. First we fell victims to the Gas Officer, by whom we were introduced to the latest pleasantries in his particular line of business, then breathlessly we marched off to listen to a most amusing and bloodthirsty lecture on Bayonet Fighting by Lieut. Colonel R. Campbell. Again we doubled in our tracks to a demonstration of the latest methods in rapid wiring by an R.E. Company, from which we only escaped in time to take part in a Tactical Exercise. In addition, we were endeavouring to carry through a series of range practices; to train Lewis gunners to man the twenty additional guns which were one day dumped outside our front door; to provide bathing times for the men; to put the Battalion through Gas Chambers, and finally to read and digest a selection of the countless pamphlets whose bulk and numbers required a limbered waggon to transport them from Brigade to Battalion Headquarters.

There was also one entire day given over to a display of concentrated Frightfulness, when we were introduced to such things as Gas Attacks, Liquid Fire, and other items calculated on first acquaintance to cause a certain shakiness of the knees. On another day the majority of the officers of the Division were taken in motor lorries to the town of Aire to hear two lectures. The lectures were somewhat dull, but the interest of the day was, however, saved by the fact that Field-Marshal Sir Douglas Haig happened to be in Aire, and came up to the Town Hall to say a word of welcome on our arrival in France. We were all intensely struck by the appearance of the Commander-in-Chief. His face was lined and gray, his shoulders bent forward, and he spoke with the voice of a wearied man. His whole presence seemed to reflect the cares and anxieties of the past weeks. The town of Aire boasts a fine open Place and stately Cathedral, but its broken buildings and torn streets showed evidences of German bombs and shells.

News soon reached us that the Division was now to take its place in the line, and we learned that our destination was Vimy Ridge, where we were to take over from a Division of the Canadian Corps. On the morning of the 8th May we left

Glomenghen and entrained at Aire. The railway line for part of the way ran within range of the German big guns, and gaping shell-holes dotted the ground by the side of the line. In the afternoon we reached a siding at Acq, where we detrained and marched to a little wood near Mont St. Eloi, whose battered tower was visible about a mile away. Here we rested until dusk. The 155 and 157 Brigades had already taken over the line below Vimy Ridge from the Canadians, and our own Brigade for the first week was to be in support. Two Battalions with Brigade Headquarters were to camp near the village of Mont St. Eloi, and the 8th Scottish Rifles, with the remaining Battalion, was to occupy some hutments at Neuville St. Vaast, which lay at the side of the main road, and about three miles nearer the line.

At dusk we set out, and marching with Platoons at 100-yard distances, reached our very brokendown and scattered camp in the darkness and without incident. The move so far sounds a straightforward business, but to avoid any suggestion of tediousness, the usual constant changes of Orders had been introduced, and in the end, when we reached our huts, we found them still in the firm possession of other troops. However, knowing that the best method of inducing workmen to leave a house is to settle down in it yourself, we put the same process into practice, and within a wonderfully short time were left in undisputed possession. Next morning Orders reached us stating that the Battalion was to return with all haste to Mont St. Eloi. Within two hours we were again on the road, and by early afternoon had settled down in another hutted camp situated almost under the shadow of the Mount.

These sudden changes of plan were explained by the fact that the Higher Command was extremely anxious regarding an expected German attack, which was believed to have the object of breaking through our lines south of Lens and north of Arras, and cutting out the Vimy sector without having to resort to a frontal attack. So the Battalion had been brought back to a position from which it could move at a moment's notice to support either flank. Our limbers were loaded and ready, and every officer and man slept in his clothes. Reconnaissances of the support lines in the Ecurie district were carried out and all preparations were made to meet any emergency. Nothing however occurred, and as the days passed the strong " breeze " which had arisen gradually died away.

On the 13th May Hume Gore and I visited the line, going the greater part of the way by motor, and before starting called at Brigade Headquarters, where we found Colonel Findlay sitting at breakfast. He had followed us from Egypt, and that morning had caught up with the Brigade. As he was still having trouble with his knee, which had been damaged by the fall from his horse, it was arranged that he should forthwith go on leave and not accompany the Battalion on its first tour in the line. From Mont St. Eloi the ground shows a gradual rise for five miles and then drops sharply at Vimy Ridge, from the top of which a wonderful view unfolds itself toward the east. Near Neuville

St. Vaast a line of white chalk hillocks marks the gaping mine craters where ran the original German line. In April, 1917, the Canadians, by a great feat of arms, pushed the German line right back over the Ridge and across some three miles of the open country beyond.

As we passed up the road we could see—now overgrown with rank grass and weeds—the long communication trenches which in these days had stretched across the miles of upland to our front line. At La Targette corner the traffic-control man on point duty waved us on, and after passing all that remains of Neuville St. Vaast, we turned to the left at the Canadian Monument and the car stopped at the roadside behind a long canvas screen of camouflage. Here and there the broken trunk of a tree showed itself, and the whole surface of the ground was torn with an unending series of shell-holes. On all hands was nothing but complete chaos and the bleakest desolation.

We were now within half a mile of the crest of the Ridge, and after passing the entrance to that vast underground system known as Thelus Caves, we entered Mersey Alley—a communication trench which formed one of the principal arteries to the front line. About here was our main Gun Line, for the country just behind the Ridge supplied hiding-places for countless batteries. When we reached the crest we climbed over the side of the trench and looked out over the open country and the maze of our trenches lying below. The German guns were busily searching our communication trenches, and when we reached the level ground below the Ridge broken duck-boards and tumbled-in trenches showed at different points that the shooting had been accurate. In Palestine we had thought that a communication trench three hundred yards long was distinctly unusual, but these were a mere hop-step-and-leap compared with the interminable miles of trench and duck-board which led to the line in front of Vimy.

The day was very hot, and we were thankful to reach the journey's end at Battalion Headquarters of the 4th K.O.S.B., which occupied a deep and extensive dug-out in a locality known as The Beehive. After we had made arrangements for the Relief on the 15th May and lunched in the splinter-proof Mess by the side of the main trench we retraced our steps to Thelus Caves, where we had tea with the Headquarters Staff of the 155 Brigade. These caves were large enough to house a complete Battalion, and the Mess where we were entertained was at least fifty feet below the surface of the ground, and lit by electric light. Later on we returned to Mont St. Eloi by motor.

Leave for the Army in France had been stopped during the previous two months, but in view of the impossibility of granting much in the way of home leave to troops in Palestine, special privileges were granted to the 52nd Division when it reached France. It was, however, made a first consideration that each Battalion when in the line must have a certain fixed establishment, and it was no small task to find the requisite numbers for the line and at the same time to make use of our modest daily leave allotment.

FRANCE

The Relief on the 15th May was to be by daylight, and in the course of the forenoon the Battalion was taken by motor lorries as far as Neuville St. Vaast. Our cookers had preceded us to this point, and a meal was ready. From here the Companies moved up with Platoons at 100-yard distances, and with the exercise of care and a little luck the Relief was carried through without a single casualty. During the seven days we spent in the line constant scares and very definite reports from higher quarters of impending German attacks kept us much on edge, but in reality the week passed quietly. Our activities consisted of sending out two patrols each night, but we never experienced anything in the nature of a real scrap with the Boche.

The question of rations and water provided a constant and unexpected source of anxiety, for with our departure from Palestine we had thought that water difficulties at least would be a thing of the past. Rations were drawn each day by Ollernshaw and arranged at the Transport Lines into sacks ready for distribution to each Platoon in the trenches. Along with the water they were brought up nightly on a light railway to a dump about half a mile behind Battalion Headquarters, the water being transported in petrol tins. The Dump at which the train dropped our supplies was shelled nightly—a fact which added to the difficulties of the parties who carried them to the forward trenches. Information reached us that on a particular night gas would be discharged from our line, and on that occasion no rations or water would come up. The exact time of this attack could not itself be fixed long beforehand, as success would depend entirely on selecting a night when wind and weather might be favourable. We had therefore to scrape together a sufficient reserve of water to carry us through a dry twenty-four hours, and rationing was brought to fine art.

Our dug-out, which had been built by the enemy before he was driven from it by the Canadians, was a perfect rabbit warren, and held the entire personnel of Battalion Headquarters. A sloping entrance led down about seventeen feet to a central hall, off which ran the Orderly-room, the Signallers' quarters and a long gallery capable of holding the remaining details. A sleeping bunk of wire-netting, stretched between wooden supports, was provided for every one of the sixty odd dwellers in the dug-out. In addition, there was a room which held bunks for five officers. The atmosphere was distinctly damp and musty, and candles supplied the only illumination. At night, during the few hours when sleep was a possibility, the rats held high carnival, and scurried over the bunks and floor or squeaked and scraped behind the logs which formed the walls and supported the roof.

We were light sleepers in these days, and could hear the jangle of equipment as the Reliefs for the Gas Sentries stumbled in the darkness up toward the two entrances of the dug-out, and at times could catch a voice from the Signal Office gabbling to a familiar Spirit of "pip don" or "ack emma." In a few minutes this recital would be followed by the arrival of a Signaller at my bedside, with a

FRANCE

stump of candle in his hand, thrusting a piece of pink paper toward me. The purport of the message would no doubt be an exhortation to search the Battalion diligently for men who in private life were Bird Fanciers, and having found them to despatch two forthwith to attend a course for Pigeoneers. On the other hand, the urgent message might seek our valued opinion as to whether the withdrawal of one pair of spurs from Transport Sections would be likely to imperil the efficiency of the British Army

The weather during our tour in the line was warm and sunny. A peep over the side of the trench showed nothing but a vast sea of twisted wire entanglements, which stretched out at all angles and in every direction as far as the eye could reach. "Stand To" was at 3 a.m., and we had daily opportunities of watching a wonderful sunrise and incidentally admiring the size and numbers of the rats which scurried about the trenches like young dogs.

Usually the day was ushered in by some of our planes flying far out over the German lines and dropping their signal balls of brilliant red or green, which floated buoyant in the air. Then the guns on either side would open up the morning "hate," and we watched with some anxiety the shell-bursts dotting perilously near one or other of our Company Headquarters. Farther to the right the unmistakable "pop" of gas shells drifted toward us. Then an unusually daring Hun plane would fly along our front trenches, and draw upon itself the "rat-tat" of our Lewis Guns as well as the attentions of one of our airmen, whose tracer bullets sent a silver stream raining on the enemy machine. Next the "Archies" would swell the chorus and bits of shrapnel begin to fall in the trenches round Battalion Headquarters. Finally the forward gun of a Field Battery would waken up and bark incessantly from its hiding-place beside two broken trees not far away. At night the gunners had little rest, and the air vibrated with the crash of shell-bursts or the lazy whine of the "heavies" on their journey to the back area. Such was the daily routine.

In those days the popular military cry was all for "Defence in depth," which meant that our front line was only held in sufficient strength to break up and disorganise an enemy attack which, if successful in penetrating the forward positions, would break its waves in vain against the succeeding and stronger defensive lines. This was no doubt a sound military doctrine, but if you yourself happened to be one of the meagre garrison in the front line with orders to hold the position to the last, and expected each night to be in the thick of a German attack, then you might become conscious of a certain feeling of loneliness.

All this time we had a spate of visitors from the Staff, and Carswell, as Mess President, was called upon to supply many extra lunches. Unfortunately on our way to the line our Mess basket, which contained all our cups, dishes, knives and forks had gone astray, and all that was left to us was the tinplate, with knife and fork, which the Artillery Liaison Officer had brought with him.

FRANCE

Consequently the lunches were distinctly of the al fresco variety.

On 23rd May we were relieved by the 7th Royal Scots, and leaving two Companies behind in immediate support, with Platoons to garrison Thelus Post and Counts Wood Post on the top of the Ridge, we went back to Hills Camp at Neuville St. Vaast. Hume Gore and I followed the Companies and dined *en route* at Brigade Headquarters Mess, in the depths of Thelus Caves.

After eight days our Brigade came into Reserve, but the 8th Scottish Rifles remained in its comfortable quarters at Hills Camp. The village of Neuville St. Vaast is typical of the desolation of War. Save for the gable wall of one cottage, which still stands by the roadside, and a few heaps of broken masonry and twisted pipes, there is no sign that any village ever existed. Here and there a wandered rose shyly pushed forth its bloom from the side of a grass-grown shell-hole, as though to proclaim the site of some cottage garden which once had been its home; and everywhere around, among the shell craters, by the roadside and even among the huts of our camp, were little crosses, each bearing a tri-colour rosette, a French soldier's name, and the grand inscription, " Mort pour la Patrie " or " Mort sur le Champ D'Honneur."

I heard a story which illustrates the ravages which War had wrought at Neuville St. Vaast. One day the British Command in this section was approached by the French authorities on behalf of an old Frenchman who in the days of peace had lived at Neuville St. Vaast. When, early in the

War, the village had to be evacuated by noncombatants, this man before leaving had buried in his garden the money and valuables representing his life's savings, and he now sought permission and assistance to recover his possessions. Owing to the proximity of the enemy, who at that time still held Vimy Ridge, it was necessary that the work should be carried out under darkness, and the Frenchman was taken up to the line to point out the spot to a small party of Sappers. He arrived at the village just after dusk, but actually searched until dawn was breaking on the following morning before he was able to locate even roughly the spot where his house once had stood. He had in the end the reward, however, of carrying back with him the buried treasure.

The vicinity of Neuville St. Vaast was shelled at intervals by day and occasionally bombed by aeroplanes at night, but barring two of our horses and a water-cart, which fell victims to a high velocity shell near La Targette corner, we escaped without casualties. Not far off floated one of our captive balloons, which, along with a dozen of its friends, kept constant watch toward the east and traced out roughly the British line as it bent back south-west of Arras.

The other three Battalions were meantime further back at Mont St. Eloi, but we had the advantage at least of being left more to our own devices, while the men had an excellent Y.M.C.A. Canteen and a daily Cinema Show at Aux Reitz.

Colonel Findlay rejoined the Battalion at Hill's Camp, and we spent one interesting day carrying out a full-dress practice attack on a trench system in conjunction with eight Tanks. I accompanied the crew of one of the Tanks during the attack and learned something of its inner workings, and the deafening noise and heat when its motors drive the lumbering animal over trenches, up steep banks, and across wide shell-holes.

While we were at Neuville St. Vaast, Padre Wilson, who had served with the Battalion constantly from Gallipoli days, left to take up another appointment at Calais, and Padre Clairmonte was posted to us in his place.

On 11th June the Battalion again went up to the line and relieved the 4th K.O.S.B. in the Betty Area of the Méricourt Section. On the morning of the Relief over fifty of our men fell sick with fever and were evacuated to hospital, so our numbers for duty in the line were considerably reduced. This outbreak was the beginning of a rather alarming epidemic of fever, and each day saw an increase in the number of our sick. Battalion Headquarters occupied a dug-out of the rabbit-warren type under the railway embankment just to the north of the ruins of Vimy village, and the Companies were disposed amid the distractingly theatrical atmosphere of trenches which bore such familiar titles as Doris Keane, Teddie Gerrard, Vesta Tilley, Lily Elsie, and the like. Our Battalion Orderly Room and Officers' Mess were strong concrete emplacements which had once housed German guns. The enemy appeared to be fully aware of our presence, for occasionally with excellent shooting he managed to drop his shells so that they just cleared the embankment and fell on the other side within a few yards of Battalion Headquarters.

The usual patrols were carried out nightly, and on one occasion John Miller, the Intelligence Officer, when well out in " No Man's Land " with fifteen of his scouts, had a very narrow escape from being enveloped by a large enemy party over a hundred strong, which was apparently preparing to raid the trenches of the 2nd Scottish Rifles immediately on our left. Fortunately he was able to withdraw his patrol just in time, and from the cover of a shell-hole breathed a heavy sigh of relief as he saw the enveloping wing of the enemy party pass by a few yards in front without securing his patrol within its pincers.

The weather remained brilliantly fine, and I was often in a position to admire the sunrise at the hour of morning " Stand To," when all hands were employed in trying to transform the immediate vicinity of Battalion Headquarters into a little defensive locality of its own. On such occasions Padre Clairmonte would help me in superintending the subsequent rum issue, and later on would start out up the communication trench with a package of sandwiches in his pocket to spend the entire day with the men in the front line. During these days he must have won a valued intimacy and friendship with many a little household in a Glasgow tenement.

At this time the first small detachment from the American Army was sent to us for a few days of instruction in Observation Duties. The four men who arrived were brought to me at Battalion Headquarters, and I asked them about their military experience and duties. One of them told me he was on the staff at a Corps Headquarters, a fact which made me regard him with a certain reverence, but he then quickly added that, including the voyage to Europe, his entire military career up to that day had only lasted seven weeks. With about the same anxiety as though telling me he had left his umbrella in a railway carriage, he asked ingenuously if I could arrange to retrieve his rifle, which he had mislaid during the previous day. Just as he might forget about his lost umbrella until it began to rain, so he now began to think that a rifle might be a handy thing to have with him in the front trenches. They were, however, keen, modest and anxious to learn, and during their stay our men took them to their hearts and treated them as guests of honour.

We had a good Observation Post on the top of the railway embankment, and at nights I occasionally went up to watch the display of fireworks from the Boche trenches. All up and down the line as far as the eye could reach, the darkness was splashed with brilliant lights of all colours. No sooner had a red rocket hurled a stream of crimson rain into the night than a whole bevy of star shells burst into fairy lights high above the red. For a moment the belt of wire opposite showed clear under the glare of a white light fired from a Very Pistol, and then a green light, suspended as though from the heavens, sent back its message, and was repeated in the further distance by other rockets until the German guns barked out their acknowledgement.

On 20th June we were relieved by the 7th Royal Scots. Our Companies were disposed at different points in immediate support, and Battalion Headquarters moved to a very delightful spot in a little wood on the top of the Ridge. The trees had suffered many casualties from shell fire, but the undergrowth was thick and leafy, and quite sufficient to hide our few "Elephant" huts and dug-outs. This was the season for wild strawberries, and the Padre, accompanied by his faithful henchman Tees, employed part of his time most usefully in supplying the Mess with a daily basket of fruit.

We were lucky in avoiding the attentions of the German Artillery, for though the daily and nightly bombardment rained down on the trenches in front or the areas behind, and other woods near at hand were nightly drenched with gas, we enjoyed almost a complete immunity. The epidemic of trench fever was still at its height, and so many officers were laid low that for two days I was the only occupant of the Mess. On one afternoon I accompanied Stanley Smith to two of the Observation Posts, which were hidden away at different points along the ridge. The afternoon light fell on the German lines, making visibility particularly good, and with the aid of the powerful telescope we could study the country far behind the front trenches. At one point I saw smoke rising from a train, and was told that as a result of constant observation the men on duty had actually been able to compile a

FRANCE

time-table for the trains which used the railways behind the German line.

On the evening of 26th June Padre Clairmonte went back to dine at Brigade Headquarters, and had not returned by the time I retired to my shack. During these days I was anxiously looking forward to my first Home Leave, and hoped to occupy one of the seats in the motor car which was to take the Brigadier to Boulogne on 1st July *en route* for home. When I was called to the telephone about 11 p.m. on this night I was more than surprised to be asked by Bruce Allan to give a message to the Colonel that the Brigadier desired I should proceed on leave the following morning (27th inst.). I could wring no reason out of Allan for this unusual request, but was told that on his return Padre Clairmonte would bring the Colonel important news which had just reached Brigade Headquarters.

When I arrived at the C.O.'s hut with my message the Padre was already there, and I heard the very sad news that the Brigades of the 52nd Division, following the arrangement in all Divisions in France, were to be reduced to three Battalions each, and that the 8th Scottish Rifles, being the Junior Battalion of the 156 Brigade, was to be transferred forthwith to a new Division. It meant nothing less than leaving behind us very many good friends and comrades and being driven forth from our home in the 52nd Division and the big family of the 156 Brigade. Even in the midst of receiving this news the Brigadier had not forgotten such a trivial affair as my Home Leave, and in case the bustle of moves and reorganisation might have meant its postponement, had expressed the wish that I should proceed on the following morning. The Colonel gave his sanction, and on the morning of the 27th I set out with David Hannan for home. On the way down to the station at Mont St. Eloi I lunched at Brigade Headquarters and said my farewells. The same night found us in the Officers' Club at Boulogne, and next morning we crossed to Folkestone in the Special Leave Boat, which carried the most care-free and cheerful crowd of passengers I have ever seen.

The following Order and Letter of Farewell were received by the Battalion on leaving the 52nd (Lowland) Division and the 156 Infantry Brigade:

(1) Order by Major-General John Hill, C.B., etc., Commanding 52nd (Lowland) Division:

"To Lieut.-Colonel J. M. Findlay, D.S.O., the Officers, Warrant Officers, N.C.O.'s and men of the 1/8th Battn. the Cameronians (Scottish Rifles)."

"It is with the greatest regret that I have to write you this farewell order.

Though I have only been associated with you as your Divisional Commander for the past 10 months, I have had ample time to judge of your splendid behaviour both in billets and in the field.

From Nov. 7th till Dec. 23rd, 1917, you were called upon almost every day to take part in some offensive operation against the Turk, and on every occasion you showed the magnificent fighting quality you possessed.

You are now going to another division and so are lost to the 52nd (Lowland) Division, but I can assure you that I, and all the Officers and men of the Lowland Division, will watch your further movements with the greatest confidence and interest.

You and the other two Battalions leaving this

division will probably be formed into a Brigade. I want you never to forget that you once belonged to the 52nd (Lowland) Division.

Goodbye, and the very best of good luck is the wish of your very grateful Divisional Commander."

    (Sgd.)   JOHN HILL, Major-General,

                              Comd. 52nd (Lowland) Division.

26th June, 1918.

(2) Letter from Brig.-Gen. A. H. Leggett, C.M.G., D.S.O., Comd. 156 Infantry Brigade, and included here by permission of Lieut.-Col. J. M. Findlay, D.S.O.:

                            HEADQUARTERS,
                            156 BRIGADE.

"MY DEAR FINDLAY,

The circumstances under which you and your Battalion are leaving us prevent me, for obvious reasons, from issuing what I much wished to issue, namely, a Special Brigade Order of the Day.

I cannot let you leave us, however, without letting you know how grieved and distressed I am that the requirements of the moment necessitate your leaving the 52nd Division, thereby depriving all of us of many a friend and this Brigade of a splendid fighting Battalion.

From Gallipoli Days right through to the present time under your gallant and fearless Leadership, the Officers and men of the 1/8th Scottish Rifles have ever proved themselves second to none whenever great hardships had to be endured and whenever hard fighting had to be done. It is not too much to say that by the dauntless courage and dash displayed in every action in which your Battalion has taken part, you its leader, and all your gallant Officers and men, have still further enhanced the great and glorious reputation of your Regiment, and done much to make the high reputation which the Brigade enjoys to-day.

Any words of mine are quite inadequate to convey to you and your lads, the intense gratitude I have toward you all for your great services to me and the Brigade. I thank you with all my heart for what you have done. I shall be grateful if you will let it be clearly understood that the new Brigade, of which you are to form a part has been formed from the Junior Battalions of each Brigade in this Division. The orders concerning this came from higher authority, were definite and final, and consequently could not be questioned.

I know that the disappointment you all feel is necessarily bound to be great, but I can assure you it is equalled by the disappointment and regret we all have at losing you.

Speaking for myself, and on behalf of the whole Brigade, I now wish you farewell and all possible good luck in the days to come.

We shall, I trust, ever keep in touch with you, and you with us. We shall follow your fortunes with the greatest interest and affection, and know that whatever you are called upon to do or face in the future, you will do as well and as gloriously as you have ever done in the past."

Always,

Yours very sincerely,

(Sgd.) A. H. LEGGETT, Brig.-General,
Comdg. 156 Inf. Bde.

28*th June*, 1918.

On 11th July I rejoined the Battalion at Cormette Camp, some four miles from St. Omer. During the period of my absence the Battalion had moved up by motor lorry to the Poperinghe Sector

FRANCE

in Flanders, and had become one of the units of the 34th Division. Along with the other two Battalions which had been taken from the 52nd Division—the 5th K.O.S.B., commanded by Dick Coulson, and the 5th A. & S.H.—we formed the 103 Infantry Brigade. The Division was commanded by Major-General C. L. Nicholson, C.B., C.M.G., and our own Brigade by Brigadier-General J. G. Chaplin, D.S.O.

On the morning of the 13th July the Brigade marched to St. Omer, and entrained at 10 a.m. for Proven. Our Transport moved by road, and the three Battalions were conveyed in one long train of covered trucks of the " 8 Chevaux 40 Hommes " type. Just as entrainment was about to begin a Hun plane hovered for some time above the station and caused us a few moments of anxiety, but the concentrated fire of several " Archies " drove the stranger off to seek its interests elsewhere.

It was a leisurely trip, and we reached Proven at 1.30 p.m. Our Camp was near the station, and was composed of tents and huts. Battalion Headquarters were in a farmhouse, where we had a very cosy little Mess. We were at that time one of the Divisions in G.H.Q. Reserve, and being under the direct orders of General Headquarters, were required to be ready to move at three hours' notice to any part of the line.

On the night of the 14th, when the Brigadier and Black, the Staff Captain, had been our guests at dinner, we experienced quite a heavy bombing attack from a number of enemy planes. It is a most unhappy sensation to hear the hum of the bombing machines as they cruise in the darkness overhead, the horrid whistle of the bombs as they cleave the air, and the earth-shaking concussion of the explosions. Fortunately our Camp did not suffer, but a gable of the Brigade House in the village was hit, and the house narrowly escaped complete destruction.

Before we had arrived at Proven there had been a spell of torrential rain, which gave us a very fair idea of the capabilities of Flanders mud, but fine weather had come again, and the ground of the Camp became rather less like a morass.

It seemed likely that in the ordinary course the 34th Division would shortly take over a part of the line in the Poperinghe Section, and we received orders to carry out a series of reconnaissances of the various support and switch systems in that region. Almost since the date of our arrival in France there had been expectations that the Germans would soon attempt another Grand Attack in the hope of forcing a final decision before the daily increasing numbers of the American Army could bring an overwhelming accession of strength to the Allies. However, the weeks and months had passed and the great effort of the enemy had not yet materialised.

On the morning of the 15th July, when some of our officers were on the point of setting out on a reconnaissance, the Brigadier walked over to our Camp and told us that in the early hours of that morning the Germans had opened their long expected attack over an eighty kilometre front on the French Sector east from Chateau Thierry and

FRANCE

Rheims; that the French had successfully withstood the weight of the first assault and, what was of greatest moment to ourselves, that our Division had been ordered south immediately to take part with the French in the grand counter attack. Plans for further reconnaissances were at once cancelled, and I spent a busy hour with the arrangements for the move.

On the same afternoon the first units of the Division left by strategical trains for the south, but our own entrainment was not due to take place till the early hours of the 17th. On the preceding evening, when the finishing touches had been put to our plans, I dined with the Colonel and Hume Gore at the " Savoy " restaurant in Proven, where we had an excellent meal.

Owing to a delay on the railway our start on the morning of the 17th was postponed by six hours, and we marched out of our Camp at the reasonable hour of 7.30 a.m. Our train could only accommodate Battalion Headquarters and three Companies along with the Transport, so " X " Company was detailed to follow by a later train. The point of entrainment was Waayenburg, a small station about two miles distant, with the huts of a large Belgian Hospital lying close at hand. Entrainment was speedily carried through, and we steamed off about 11 a.m. Corporal M'Donald, with Mess basket in charge, had dealt out a supply of rations to the compartment which I shared with the Colonel and Hume Gore, and we settled down to make the best of the trip. There was an undoubted air of excitement throughout the whole

Battalion, and there was certainly plenty of scope for rumour and imagination, for barring a rough guess that our immediate destination was to be Châlons-sur-Marne, about seventy miles east of Paris, we had no definite information of any kind. Hume Gore again proved his prowess with a tin-opener, and we spent a wonderfully comfortable day and night in the train.

We had expected to spend two nights *en route*, but as we came to a halt at Chantilly Station shortly after 1 p.m. on the 18th, we noticed transport waggons on the sidings bearing the chequer-board sign of the 34th Division, and some of our Divisional Staff waiting on the platform. We then realised that we were nearing the end of our train journey, and learned that our point of detrainment would be at Survilliers, a station some few miles further south.

Half an hour later we reached our destination, and after dinners had been taken at the station, the Battalion set out by march route for the village of Balagny, a distance of some thirteen miles. The road led us for several miles through the Forest of Chantilly, and at points where the forest tracks branched out from the main road we had wonderful views of leafy vistas and dark silent glades. Soon we passed a Brigade of our Artillery bivouacked by the roadside, and just as dusk was setting in we marched up the long cobbled main street of Senlis. This town represented the high water mark of the German invasion of 1914, and there could be no better incentive to the spirit of revenge than to march through its streets before coming to grips

with the Hun, for every house on both sides of
the road had been wantonly destroyed by fire. As
we passed up the street a few French urchins played
by the gutter, but otherwise there were few signs
of life, and on all hands stood nothing but black
and charred ruins. One large house had been
saved from destruction, and I noticed a Red Cross
flag fluttering from its roof.

Leaving Senlis on our left, we struck out to the
east, and at 10 p.m. we came to the end of our
march and reached Balagny. This was nothing
but a diminutive village standing well back off
the main road, and when I walked down to the
village square I found it still full of French
Cavalry. However, after finding the Maire, we
learned that the present tenants were on the point
of leaving, and that the village was at our disposal.
Meantime we could see nothing of Russell, who
had gone on ahead with a small billeting party, but
we eventually ran against his spoor in the white
chalk figures on the doors of the houses. Billeting
in the dark and in a village which none of us had
seen before was not easy, and to make matters
worse, the approach of a flight of Hun planes bent
on a bombing expedition made the use of lights
very inadvisable. However, by 1 a.m. the Battalion had settled down, and in the room of an
empty house Corporal M‘Donald had produced for
us a scratch meal consisting of bread and jam, with
champagne of a sweet and sticky character.

The German planes were busy meantime
dropping their bombs, while the beams of many
searchlights swept the sky and the shrapnel of the

Sketch Map of ——
VIMY DISTRICT

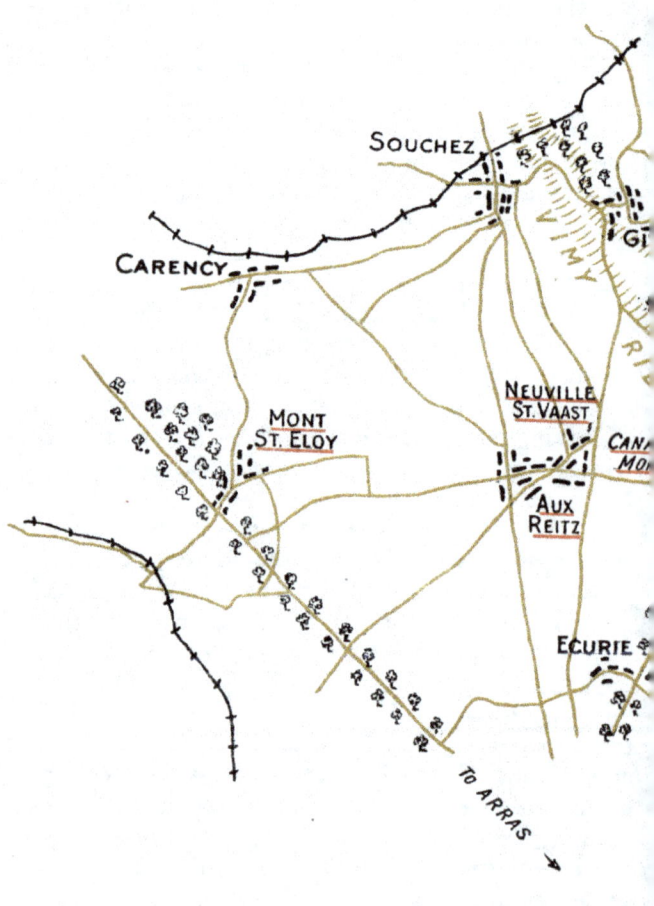

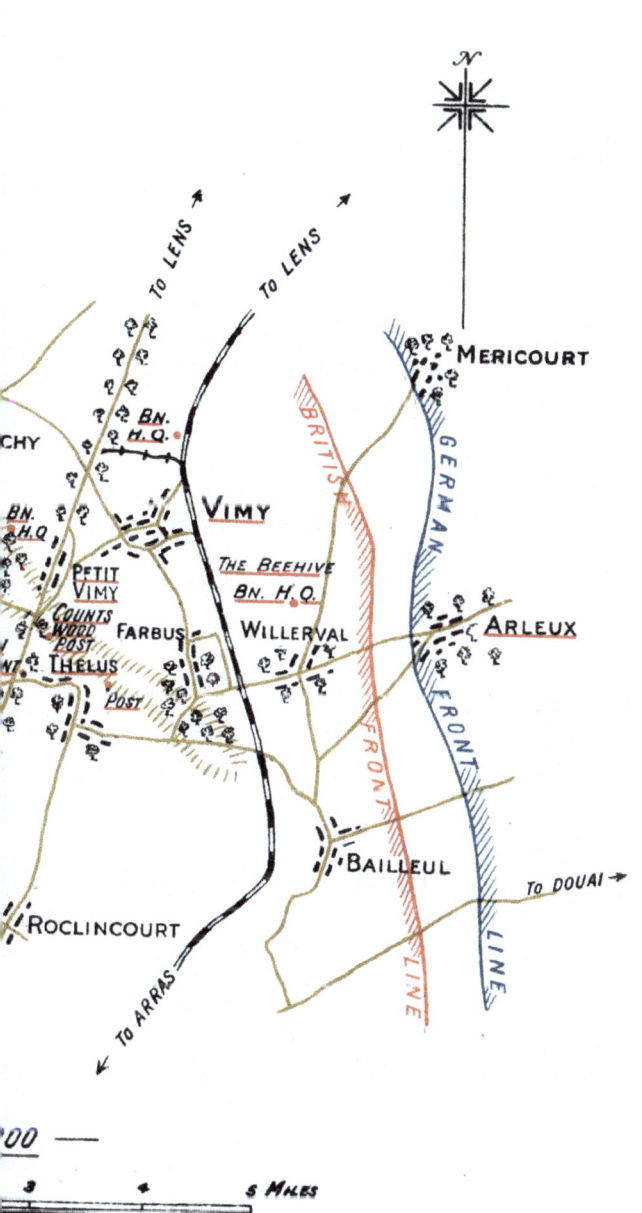

"Archies" burst overhead like the twinkling of stars. In spite of these distractions, the meal was very welcome, and it was consumed in the brilliant light of one candle, standing in its own grease on the mantelpiece with its small flicker of light almost entirely hidden by two steel helmets. Then I found the little house in which Hume Gore and I had each managed to secure a bed, and taking off my tunic and boots, fell asleep.

Twice during the next few hours messages from Brigade Headquarters were brought to me, and on both occasions I had to take them over to the Colonel, whose billet was about a hundred yards away. A third message reached me at 6.55 a.m. on the 19th, and contained orders for the Battalion to em-bus at a point on the road a mile distant at 7 a.m. This seemed to be rather out of the question, and it was essential too that the men should be allowed time to have their breakfasts, which were now ready.

Our departure was a hurried affair, for within a very short time we were on the road, and soon found the long line of waiting motor lorries. An empty feeling in my inside reminded me that I had failed to get any breakfast, but the noble Pryer had filled my Thermos flask with hot tea, for which act I freely blessed him. The lorries belonged to the French Army and were driven by Frenchmen, and the convoy was in charge of a French officer, who rode in front in a motor car, in which the Colonel and I were invited to join him.

Our route took us again through the outskirts of Senlis, and then east by the main road. Of all crowded thoroughfares I have seldom seen anything to equal the traffic that passed up and down on this long straight road. Detachments of troops of all arms in the French, American and British Armies were there; big high-powered touring cars carrying French Staff Officers elbowed their way through the traffic; unending strings of lumbering motor lorries hurried troops and rations to the fighting zone, and from the direction of the front line countless Red Cross motor waggons carried heavy loads of bandaged French and Americans with smiling faces toward the hospitals at Senlis.

After we had covered some fifteen miles we halted owing to one of the many blocks in the traffic, and there we found the Brigadier. He pointed out a little village in which we were to billet for the night, and told us that meantime the lorries would take us further on to a point where a side road made a loop with the main road and provided a quiet backwater, where the Battalion could de-bus and have a meal.

Having considered the situation, the Colonel thought it wise to make early arrangements for billets, so taking Pryer and Tees with me, I set about returning to Russy, the village which the Brigadier had shown us and which lay a few hundred yards from the main road and about three miles back. Seeing a big French touring car carrying only one passenger coming towards us, I stopped it, and having treated the Staff Officer to a fine flow of perfect French and showed him on the map where I wanted to go, we bundled inside and started off. By great good luck the Staff Officer himself was making for our village, and there we arrived about ten minutes later.

On closer inspection the village seemed to consist of one big farm-steading and a big courtyard with one large private house, and the whole place was already packed with an assortment of French detachments which showed no signs of making a move. I then sought out the Maire, who appeared to be the Local Food Controller and was busily engaged in issuing rations of grain to the poor people, but he knew nothing of our expected arrival, and informed me politely that there was certainly no room for any additional troops. It was now about 2 p.m., and the Battalion was not likely to arrive for a few hours, so I lay down at the side of a field to consider the situation.

During the past two days we had received some scraps of news which threw a little light on the military position. The German line now formed a big salient, whose base ran between Soissons and Rheims and whose apex lay roughly at Chateau Thierry. The plan of Marshal Foch seemed to be to press in on both sides of the salient and squeeze the Boche out. To help him in the squeezing process he had, in addition to the French troops, four American Divisions and the same number of British Divisions, and of these latter, the 51st and 62nd were on the Rheims side, while the 15th and 34th were on the Soissons side. The 15th British Division was apparently to relieve the 1st American Division, which was then doing yeoman service in the line, while the rôle to be played by the 34th British Division was not yet definitely known.

FRANCE

Without doubt the situation was developing to our advantage, for everyone coming from the direction of the fighting wore a quiet smile of satisfaction. There were car-loads of heavily braided and be-medalled French Staff Officers; there were officers of the American Staff with keen, alert eyes, casting sharp glances through their pince-nez as they sped past in their new grey-green cars, which made the French and British machines look battered and worn in comparison; and there was the stream of wounded. Everywhere there was an evident feeling of optimism.

A short time later I was surprised to see Russell approaching me on a bicycle, and I at once hailed him. He had just left Rotherford the Brigade Major, and was able to tell me that plans had been changed and that the Battalion on arrival was to bivouac in a wood near by. Better still, I found that Russell had been able to procure some provisions from an American Canteen, so we sat down by the side of the main road, where we could not miss the Battalion, and did away with a tin of sardines, some bread and a tin of fruit.

It appeared that on the previous night, after arranging our billets at Balagny, Russell had expected the Battalion would detrain at Senlis, and hurried off there to receive us. But he waited all night in vain, not knowing that we had reached our destination by march route.

As we sat there watching the stream of traffic, a long column of German prisoners came down the road, with a small party of German officers in front. It was a cheering sight, and as the column halted opposite us, we were able to take good stock of the different types. They all seemed to be there, from the tall officer in front, who appeared to feel his position keenly, but endeavoured to carry it off with a certain show of swagger, to the little round fat fellow with pig-like eyes and thick spectacles, who, on the contrary, gave the impression of viewing his captivity with complete equanimity.

Later on the Battalion arrived, and we moved up a short way into the Bois de Tillet, where we found ample space in which to bivouac the Companies. The foliage in the wood was fresh and luxurious, and as the weather was fine, we were well content with our quarters. Battalion Headquarters settled down in a little open glade, and with many arrears to make up, I fell asleep, wrapt in my quilt and lying on a stretcher, to the sound of rustling leaves and with the stars peeping through the branches overhead. We were disturbed for a short time by some German aeroplanes engaged on a night bombing expedition, but our luck held, and they passed without selecting our particular wood as a target.

Early on the morning of the 20th we had a visit from the Brigadier, who told us we would spend the day in our present location and move again in the evening. At this time the officers at Battalion Headquarters were Colonel Findlay, Hume Gore, Innes, John Nicholl, John Miller of "X" Company, who was now taking his namesake's place as Intelligence Officer, Darsie, Doctor Clark, Russell, Sadler the Quartermaster, and myself.

FRANCE

We spent a restful day, and at about 6 p.m. we received preliminary orders to march at 7.40 p.m. to Feigneux, a village about two miles distant which provided accommodation for Brigade Headquarters and the 5th K.O.S.B. Further detailed orders were to follow, but as these did not arrive, we moved off at 7.40 p.m., leaving behind the nucleus under Hume Gore.

The weather, unfortunately, had shown distinct signs of a break, and as we passed out of the wood heavy rain began to fall. When we reached a point on the road near Feigneux, we were informed we would not resume the march till midnight, and the intervening hours were spent by most of us cowering by the roadside under a deluge of torrential rain, accompanied by thunder and lightning.

We also learned that we were embarking on a night march of some eighteen miles, which would bring us to the village of Soucy. Midnight saw us again on the move, and passing through Feigneux, we headed for another main road, which ran directly toward the front. For some time we made good progress, but when we reached the road junction we had a long halt to enable a Brigade of our Artillery to pass the crossing in front. I had filled my Thermos flask with hot coffee before starting, and this seemed a good time to sample it, but on opening the case I found that most of the coffee had run out, and that the metal cover was filled principally with broken glass.

The clatter of the gun wheels ahead died away, and we again started. The rain had now ceased, but the night air was damp and cold, while mud lay thick on the road. We passed through one or two dark sleeping villages, and about 6 a.m. climbed up a long steep hill into a deep forest. Just as we crossed the railway at the bottom of the hill an immense gun, mounted on railway trucks three hundred yards away, went off with a terrific report as it hurled its 15 inch shell through space to find a target behind the German line.

At other times our road through the forest would have appeared as a beautiful and altogether desirable route, but in the early hours of that morning it was merely an unending road, over whose broken and muddy surface a Brigade of weary, wet and hungry men had to pass before their resting-place could heave in sight.

At one point we met and saluted a Battalion of the 1st American Division, which had just been relieved in the line. Underneath the branches of the giant trees we could see countless encampments of Infantry and Cavalry, with whole parks of motor waggons and repair shops. At long last we marched into the village of Soucy at 9.30 a.m., having been fourteen hours on the road since leaving the Bois de Tillet.

The house allotted to Battalion Headquarters had apparently been hurriedly vacated sometime previously by its owners, and was now in an advanced condition of mess and filth. Most of the furniture was broken, every drawer had been rifled, and rags, papers and pieces of torn garments lay thick on the floor. So before settling down to sleep, we had to carry out a small Spring cleaning. It said much for the enterprise and efficiency of the Army

FRANCE 225

Postal Service that on this day, when at the end of constant moves, the Battalion seemed to have completely hidden itself behind these miles of forest, two home mails reached us. The Brigade Staff occupied a farmhouse not far away, in which Colonel Findlay also had a room, and in the evening I accompanied the Colonel to a conference with the Brigadier, when future operations and the part in the scheme assigned to the 103 Brigade were discussed. It was late when the conference ended, and after orders for the following day had been written, I turned in.

Early on the morning of the 22nd the Colonel, with Eric Findlay and M'Combie, rode off to take part in a reconnaissance of the forward positions, and the Battalion, under command of Captain Ferguson, marched out from Soucy at 9 a.m., and took its place in the Brigade column. Our way led us again through the heart of the forest. The lowest branches of the great trees spread out so high above us that there was ample head room to ride along without running the risk of emulating the misfortunes of Absalom. It was arranged that in order, so far as possible, to avoid coming under aeroplane observation, we should move under cover, and for mile after mile we marched along on the soft leafy soil in the shade of the great boughs, while the Transport moved parallel to the Battalion along the road.

At different points we saw French and American troops on the move, detachments of Cavalry and Engineers, huge ammunition dumps, guns and tanks, until the forest seemed to be hiding one vast army under its green covering. The passing of the hours and miles brought us nearer the bark of the guns, and it seemed as though we must soon be in the thick of the mêlée. At noon we halted for a short time near some units of the 15th Division, and then emerging from the Forest, we pushed on along a side road till we entered a wood near Chavigny Farm, about a mile short of the town of Longpont. Here the men had dinner, and we rested under the trees awaiting further orders.

This wood had been prepared as a defensive locality, and deep trenches and stout entanglements of wire ran through the undergrowth. From the front of the wood a long line of captive balloons floating in the air seemed to bend back on our right and left, as though we were at the very point of a salient. This may have been a delusion, but balloons always seemed to give us this impression. As we watched, a Boche airman came over and shot down the nearest balloon, which fell in a sheet of flame to the ground. Revenge for this came quickly, for a few minutes later one of the enemy balloons shared a similar fate at the hands of an Allied airman. A few shells from the German guns fell near at hand, but none reached our wood.

The Colonel had not yet returned from his reconnaissance, but a message received from Brigade Headquarters told me that since the previous night Orders had been changed, and that the 8th Scottish Rifles was now to be one of two Battalions in reserve to the French XXXth Corps, and that at

11.30 p.m. we would move again some five miles further on to a forward area. Just as it was getting dark the Colonel returned, and we prepared again to take the road. As we were now rapidly approaching the fighting zone, it was essential that we should proceed with considerable caution under cover of darkness, and at 11.30 p.m. we debouched again on to the road, moving with Platoons at 100-yard distances.

The French Ammunition Columns were busily employed in carrying up fresh supplies of shells to the guns, and we were frequently delayed by numbers of great lumbering waggons drawn by four-horse teams cutting in from side roads and causing our Companies and Platoons to run the risk of losing touch in the dark. Soon we passed through Longpont, a town of fair size, which a few days previously had been in German hands. A river runs through the town, and the stone bridge across it had been demolished by the retreating enemy, but we passed over on an excellent military bridge, which provided a good advertisement to the skill of French Engineers. A few shrapnel shells burst near the bridge during our crossing, but we escaped casualties. On the other side a steep hill carried the road across a high plateau, and after a short time we passed through the ruined village of Villers Helon.

I was riding with the Colonel at the head of the Battalion, but often had to dismount and retire to the bottom of a neighbouring shell hole to read by the light of a match the messages which reached us at intervals by Cyclist Orderly from the Brigade

Staff. The enemy guns were searching the road ahead, and it certainly added no zest to our night march to notice a profusion of shells bursting at points on the route along which we must shortly pass. Although the German Artillery fire was brisk, it was as nothing compared to the storm of shells which the French "75s" hurled at the enemy. At a pre-arranged point two French soldiers met us to guide the Battalion to the Bois du Fond de Soissons, which was to be our halting place. Soon the enemy shells began to burst nearer us, and just before reaching the village of Blanzy we moved off the main road, and followed a cart track which would take us more directly to our destination.

At this point we seemed to be surrounded by countless batteries, all firing at highest speed, and the noise and general din were indescribable. Just as the two platoons comprising Battalion Headquarters had got clear of the road a German shrapnel shell burst in the air beside us, and a splinter hit my right forearm. Fortunately no one else was damaged, and as I had very little pain, the Colonel tied up his handkerchief as a sling for my arm, and we continued on our way toward the wood. A little later we had to check our pace and halt in order not to lose touch with the Companies, and the Doctor, who had been sent for by the Colonel, made his way from his place at the rear of the Battalion to the front of the column.

Accompanied by the faithful Pryer, we went over to a French Aid Post near the edge of the wood, where, by the light of an electric torch, the Doctor slit open my sleeve and displayed a much larger wound than I had expected. After examining it, he remarked casually that it was a nice wound, not dangerous, but would keep me at home for a long time. Considering our present surroundings, the idea of "Home" took some little time to percolate through my skull. Inside the little Aid Post the beam of the electric torch showed us a crazy roof composed of two strips of corrugated iron, and on the mud floor a green fibre box filled with surgical dressings. In the corner was a stretcher on which a French Medical Orderly snored lustily. It was now 3 a.m. on the 23rd, and with the first grey lines of dawn beginning to streak the sky, a fine rain started to fall ; the wild storm of the guns thundered incessantly, and home seemed just about as near as the North Pole. And then, by way of marking the occasion, I told Pryer to bring me the flask from my haversack so that we might pour out a libation.

The Doctor was anxious I should get away as soon as possible, so I sent for my pack, which had been smuggled along in the Medical Cart, also my saddle-bag and raincoat from my horse. One or two horse-drawn ambulances carrying loads of wounded French soldiers were preparing to set out from the Aid Post for the dressing stations further back, but one of the French N.C.O.s suggested I should walk a little way to the corner of another wood, where an American motor ambulance was usually to be found. So Pryer loaded himself with most of my gear, and we set out. As we left the trees the Companies were moving up to their respective areas, and John Nicholl, having dumped the rations and water, was preparing to start with the Transport on his return journey to the wood near Longpont. The German fire seemed to increase with the dawn, but we safely reached the other wood, and eventually found the motor ambulance. The American driver was asleep at the bottom of a deep well, which served as an excellent dug-out, but I wakened him and asked to be taken to the dressing station. It was quite an exciting ride, for the Boche was still shelling the road, and we had to proceed with some caution to avoid gaping shell-holes.

We first went to a desolate, ruined village about two miles back, where there was a French Dressing Station, and having taken on board three Poilus, we continued our journey, which was to take us to Villers Cotterêts. We soon passed out of the zone of fire, and with returning day, life seemed to hold out less dismal prospects. During the ten mile run I sat in front with the driver, and had it not been for the blow of fresh air in my face, I certainly would have fallen asleep.

The country through which we passed had within the last few days been the scene of strenuous fighting, and the fields were seared with trenches and pitted with shell-holes. Eventually, at 4 a.m., we passed through Villers Cotterêts, and on the further outskirts of the town we drew up before a number of marquees which formed the Collecting Station. Next to the marquees was a siding, which served as railhead for the French ambulance trains.

FRANCE

Up to this point Pryer had accompanied me, but as he could not come further, I got him some hot coffee from the French Canteen and sent him back by the motor ambulance to report to John Nicholl at the Transport Lines. Some time afterwards I was very grieved to hear he had been killed in the fighting a few days later. He was known as "Jackie" throughout the Battalion, and was one of our most popular men. His constant cheerfulness was of the infectious kind, and at the very worst of times he could be heard unconcernedly whistling or singing a popular song. If he was not busy with his own work he was usually helping some one else. He was a good friend and comrade.

In the Collecting Station there were already many wounded Frenchmen, but so far, I was the only representative of the British Divisions. My particulars were taken by a French officer in the Reception Marquee, and I was then passed through to a portion which was screened off as a surgery. In a short time a Doctor arrived, and signed to me to loosen my clothing around my middle. I assumed he wanted to examine my wound, so I pointed instead to my arm lying in its sling. This, however, did not appear to satisfy him, and he still continued to show an anxious interest in the particular region where my only complaint consisted of a slightly empty feeling. I loosened my garments, and then noticing the Doctor fingering a large syringe, I tumbled to the fact that I was on the point of being inoculated against tetanus. I thought he took rather an unfair advantage in selecting my middle as the point at which to dig in the needle, but not wishing to endanger the *Entente* in any way, I submitted with the best grace I could command.

They were kindly souls in the Collecting Station, and soon they brought me a tin mug filled with a tepid tea substitute, and a long slice of brown bread surmounted by a pyramid of cold " Maconachie." It was not very appetising, and, as a matter of fact, I longed for sleep far more than for food, but could see no place on which to lie except a stretcher which already carried the recumbent frame of a French Colonel. I learned that an ambulance train was not expected for some hours, and just as I was trying to make myself comfortable on a narrow wooden bench, a British R.A.M.C. sergeant with two orderlies walked into the marquee. They had been sent to look after any British wounded who might be evacuated from Villers Cotterêts, and being at that moment their only charge, I was able to make full use of their services. I told the sergeant I had a great desire to lie down, and though he could find nothing in the shape of either a bed or a stretcher, he returned with three good planks of wood. We laid these along the side of the marquee, and having told him to wake me when the train came in, I wrapped my quilt round me, hitched my pack under my head, and having arranged my arm in the least uncomfortable position, fell asleep.

The events of the night had moved so quickly and unexpectedly that I hardly realised I was now actually away from the Battalion and the immediate scenes of war, and I certainly never guessed that my Active Service career was at an end. No doubt a History of the Battalion will recount day by day the part it played in the remaining stages of the Great Game, but all the world knows the general result of the fighting in the salient south of Soissons, and how the success of the counter attack, which was there set on foot by French, American and British Forces, widened out and gathered momentum until in the end the Armistice gave the Boche the only chance which could save his armies from utter annihilation.

When the day came on which the British Divisions were brought out of the line to rejoin our Armies in the North, the French soldiers selected a commanding site and raised there a rough monument to the memory of the Scottish Troops who had been engaged, and many of whom were now sleeping their last sleep among the woods and valleys of that beautiful country. The memorial may have been rough, but no sentiment was ever more perfect than was expressed in the words cut upon its base:

"*The Thistles of Scotland will for ever bloom amid the Roses of France.*"

The whole operations on the west side of the salient had been under the direction of the French General, Mangin, and the following is the Order of the Day which at their close he addressed to the British Divisions under his command:

"You came into the battle at its fiercest moment. The enemy, defeated the first time, brought up against us his best Divisions in numbers superior to

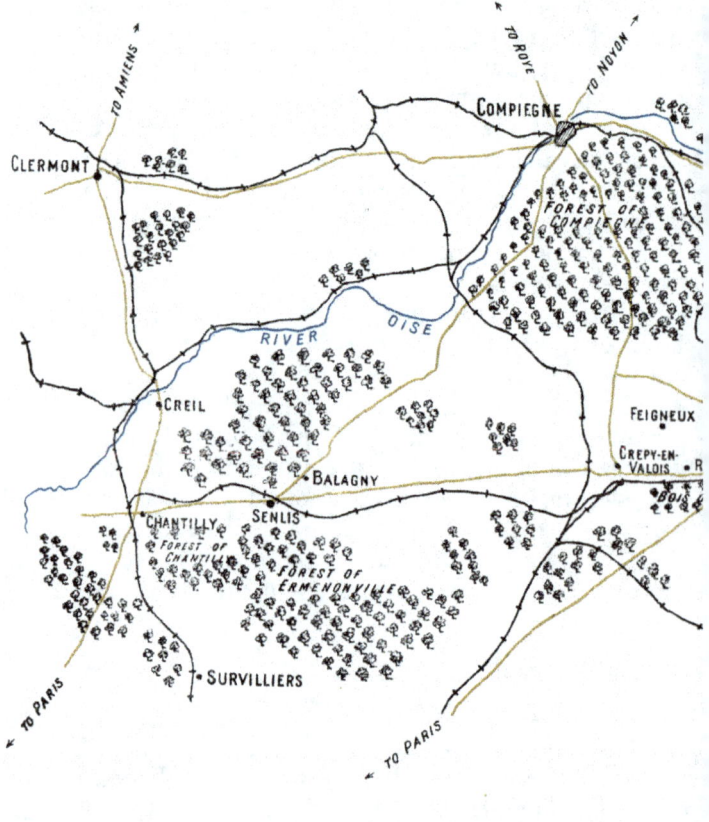

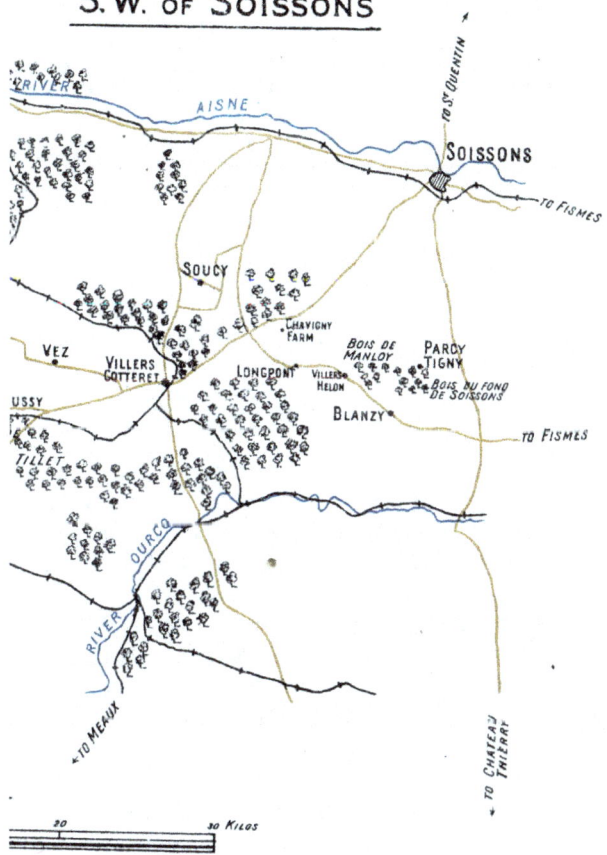

our own. You continued to advance foot by foot in spite of his bitter resistance, and you held on to the conquered ground notwithstanding the violence of his counter attacks. Then on August 1st, side by side with your French Comrades, you carried the height dominating the Country between the Aisne and the Ourcq, which the defenders had been ordered to hold at all costs. Having failed in his attempts to retake the height with his last reserves, the enemy was compelled to retreat, pursued and harrassed for a distance of 12 kilometres (about seven miles). All you English and Scottish troops, both the young soldiers and the veterans of Flanders and Palestine, have shown the magnificent qualities of your race— namely, indomitable courage and tenacity. You have won the admiration of your brothers-in-arms. Your country will be proud of you, for to you and to your Commanders is due in large measure the victory which we have just gained against the barbarous enemies of all free peoples. I am happy to have you under my Command, and I thank you."

After what seemed to me to be about five minutes time, but was in reality four hours, my friend the R.A.M.C. Sergeant wakened me and told me the ambulance train was in the station. So we gathered my belongings together, and walked along to the officers' coach. During the hours I had been asleep a number of other wounded from our Division had drifted to the Collecting Station, and I also saw some German wounded prisoners, who had received medical attention, being helped along to the train. I was the only British officer in the coach, and the remaining occupant was a French Captain of Artillery, whose head was swathed in bandages. The coach was an

FRANCE

ordinary covered truck with big doors, which opened at the middle of each side, but it differed from the usual troop train truck, in that it was spotlessly clean. In three of the corners were slung tiers of three stretchers, while the fourth corner held a table with some dishes and other odds and ends. The French Captain was a good fellow and most friendly, but unfortunately his knowledge of English was strictly limited, while my vocabulary of French did not extend very far beyond the bounds of that interesting and instructive little poem, entitled "Le Corbeau et Le Renard."

However, we got on very well, and before the train had started we had smoked each other's cigarettes and established relations on a sound and friendly basis. I had still many arrears to make up, so lay down in great comfort on one of the stretchers and fell asleep. About midday I was wakened by my friend with the cheerful greeting, "Will Monsieur eat?" I replied at once, "Certainly Monsieur will eat," and on getting up I saw that the attendant had arranged a table with two chairs between the wide open doors, and that déjeuner was ready. I found I was thoroughly hungry, and we had an excellent meal of soup, omelette and stew, with some good red wine. When we reached the coffee stage the attendant produced a bottle which he explained was his own personal property, and poured out for each of us a small glass of quite palatable liqueur brandy.

The train moved along in leisurely fashion, and it was very pleasant to sit lazily by the open door looking out on quiet fields and rivers and woods.

We occasionally stopped at stations, where some of the wounded were taken from the train, but no one appeared to know our final destination and no one seemed much to care. I had lain down again on the stretcher, and must have dozed off, for I was wakened a second time by the French Officer, who varied his greeting on this occasion by asking, "Will Monsieur drink?" So again I got up and said "Certainly Monsieur will drink." He then took me along to the corridor carriage where the Medical Staff lived, and in the compartment used as their mess he introduced me to two Doctors and the Colonel whose snores I had heard coming from the stretcher at the Collecting Station.

From the bottle which stood on the table one of the Doctors poured out and handed me a small glass of a liqueur, which I realised later was a fiery relative to White Mint, and then from the short speech he made I gathered he was inviting the party to drink to the health and prosperity of the British Army. It was the first time I had found myself called upon to represent the five or six million men of our Army scattered throughout every theatre of War, but I had a feeling that something was now demanded of me. It was not such a difficult matter to conjure up the sentiments suitable to the occasion, but in vain I mentally searched each line of "Le Corbeau et Le Renard" to lay my hands on the appropriate words in which to express them. In the end I shirked the attempt and fell back upon the less adventurous "Vive La France!" at the same time quaffing the remains of the liqueur, which incidentally nearly choked me as it trickled down to my vitals like a torchlight procession. Then I remembered my flask, in which there was just enough whisky left to give each the smallest taste, but it seemed to please them mightily, and they sipped it as though it were the Nectar of the Gods, and the *entente* flourished exceedingly.

It was now nearly 6 p.m., and although for some hours we had been travelling toward the north, none even yet seemed to know our destination. I was particularly anxious to find my way either to a British or American Hospital, and realised that the further we went toward the north the better was my chance.

A little later we stopped at a large town, and my friend the Captain approached me with the well-known and excellent formula on his lips, "Will Monsieur eat?" It seemed a good opportunity for dinner, so we were led through the midst of an admiring throng on the platform to the Station Restaurant, where we had a first-rate meal. One of the courses consisted of an excellent omelette, and with a particularly fine linguistic effort I politely remarked that they made much better omelettes in France than in Britain. I must have got a bit wide of my mark, for the meaning which I apparently succeeded in conveying to my friend was that I thought the French Army far superior to the British Army. This annoyed me exceedingly, for even the wildest flights of international courtesy could not have dragged from me such an opinion. His politeness, however, was equal to the task, and he refused to agree, although he mentioned, as possible grounds for my assertion, that before the War the numbers of the French Army were very large compared to ours, and that even in days of peace the French had large permanent Staffs. In desperation I felt that something must be done at once to correct his impressions, and after further liberties with his native tongue and numerous stabs with my fork at the unoffending omelette on my plate, I succeeded in driving my meaning home. Then he laughed heartily, and all was well.

Knowing that I had a little money still in my pocket and wishing to show some small appreciation for all his kindness, I had ordered a bottle of good wine, but when I went to the cash desk to settle up before returning to the train, the attendant would accept nothing, either for the dinner or the wine, for, as my Captain explained, we were the guests of the State.

When the train started again I was able to find out that our destination was Rouen, where we were due at 9 p.m., and being rather ignorant of the medical dispositions of our Army, I wondered if I would have the luck to find a British hospital. When we eventually steamed into the station I had my head well out of the window to try to catch sight of anyone in a British uniform, and, to my great joy, I saw on the platform an R.A.M.C. Sergeant and one or two privates. The Sergeant must have been attracted by my Balmoral bonnet, for as the train stopped he came straight up to me and asked if I was Captain Boyd. Here was evidence of the finest Staff work, and after saying

FRANCE

good-bye to my friends of the ambulance train, I was taken to a motor car and in five minutes found myself at the entrance porch of No. 2 British Red Cross Hospital.

It was now 9.30 p.m., and when I reached my ward I found that things there had settled down for the night. The Night Sister was a good-hearted soul from Aberdeen, and to her I made a strong and successful appeal that I should forthwith have a hot bath. An orderly appeared, who helped me to remove my gory raiment and directed the bathing operations. Then having swallowed a cup of hot tea, I had the delightful sensation of going to sleep in a comfortable bed between cool white sheets. So much had happened since I had been wounded, and I was now so far from the Battalion that it was difficult to realise it was still the same day.

Next morning I was wakened by the Sister, who was engaged in pushing a thermometer well down my throat, and after breakfast the white-coated Surgeon came to the ward on his morning rounds. I was rather disappointed with the apparent lack of interest he seemed to display in my wound, which personally I had been thinking was quite a respectable looking gash, for after a hasty glance at it he murmured something about " cleaning it out," and promptly pushed into it a large wad of absorbent cotton, well soaked in some very energetic disinfectant. This made the wound smart so acutely that I must have jumped at least a foot off the bed, but he paid no attention, and moved on to the next patient as though hopeful of finding a more interesting and unusual case. I think he was rewarded, for the man in the next bed had arrived that morning, and his whole body was covered with bandages. I suppose my own wound was just a common every day type, of which he examined several dozens each morning.

No. 2 British Red Cross Hospital had apparently in the days of peace been the home of some religious brotherhood or sisterhood. It was a fine solid stone building, excellently adapted for its present use, standing on high ground above the town, and the paved quadrangle in the middle gave additional accommodation for two large huts, which formed temporary wards. Great buttresses of sandbags lay in symmetrical piles against the walls, and arrows pointed the way toward the cellars, which would provide a safe retreat in the event of air raids. On higher ground above the Hospital stood the house of the Archbishop of Rouen, and between the two lay in terraces a fine garden, which was open at all times to the patients.

There were officers in the wards with bodies and limbs sadly shattered and maimed, or septic with gas sores, and occasionally the big double-doors of our ward would open to allow a stretcher party to carry a patient to the operating theatre, or to bring him back later a motionless figure still surrounded by the pungent smell of chloroform. In one of the smaller wards, where silence reigned, an officer was grimly fighting for his life against the poison which had grappled with his system before his wound could be tended, and in another could be heard the murmurings of delirium from a

FRANCE

patient who in subconsciousness was still leading a bombing attack against a nest of German machine guns. His bed was shut off by screens from the rest of the ward, and a Sister sat constantly by his side.

In spite of all there was a wonderful atmosphere of cheerfulness and gaiety, and in most of the wards bridge games were in progress, while overworked gramophones scraped out tit-bits of ragtime or musical comedy. Soon I learned the unwritten law enacted by the patients themselves, which provides that every officer who is sound of limb and able to move about should take his share in lightening the work of the Ward sisters and the V.A.D.s. And so it was that early each morning two officers, armed with soap and hot water, systematically washed the tops of the little wooden lockers which stood by the head of each bed. Others were engaged in collecting and polishing the brass ash-trays till they shone like mirrors, while a little group at the end of the ward was apparently overhauling the portable reading desks. Then the breakfast trays were carried round, and afterwards the ward decked itself out with pink chintz bed covers and gave itself over to the medical forms of " spit and polish " likely to find favour in the eagle eye of the Matron. No " Brass Hat " engaged in inspection duties ever instilled such awe as the Matron of the Hospital when she walked through the wards, and many Generals might have envied her the display of war ribbons which gave a touch of gaiety to her dark blue uniform.

In the evening the clang of a bell announced the arrival of another convoy of wounded, and one of the Sisters came hurriedly into the ward exclaiming in tones of enthusiasm which were certainly complimentary to the nationality of the new arrivals, "Here's an entire convoy of Jocks." A few minutes later the numbers in our ward were increased by ten. Most of them were walking cases, but a few were carried in on stretchers. The patients already there, or as many of them as could move about, were soon busy helping off muddy boots, winding up puttees, superintending at the bath, carrying cups of tea or showering cigarettes and questions on the newcomers. The American officer in the bed next to me, who had been a silent observer, turned his head in my direction and said with a wealth of feeling, "Well, I guess that's some sight." For an exhibition of comradeship, tenderness, care, and much that forms the brighter side of human nature recommend me to a Red Cross Hospital in France.

The above mentioned American officer, fearing he might be too late for the fray if he allowed events in the United States to run their course, had come over to England and joined the Royal Air Force. His fears that he might be too late for the fighting had however been groundless, for he had spent many months in France, and was now lying with a hole through his ankle, which marked the course of a bullet fired at him while he was flying low and emptying drums of cartridges from his Lewis gun along the German trenches. In a bed opposite was a Canadian officer upbraiding his luck because his wounds were not sufficiently severe to take him to England.

FRANCE

One of the super moments of my life occurred on the second afternoon of my stay, when the Surgeon came to my bed and, after looking at the chart and particulars on the board above my head, said: "I suppose you would like to go to England." I told him he had guessed right, and then he took down my board, and in hospital parlance "marked me up for Blighty."

Nothing remained now but to wait with an outward display of patience for the next convoy. It was due to leave for England early on the morning of the 27th July, and on that day at 8.30 a.m. I left Rouen on a British Hospital Train for Havre. In the afternoon we drew up alongside the docks, and boarded the Hospital Ship "Gloucester Castle." Later we moved to the outer harbour, where we remained within the boom defences until darkness fell upon the waters of the Channel. There were three Hospital Ships and one or two miscellaneous vessels in the convoy, and when we passed out through the boom-gates three British Destroyers took up their stations as our escort.

The "Gloucester Castle" was an excellent ship, and we spent a comfortable night in the swinging cots, which defy the motion of the water. Early on Sunday morning, the 28th July, we passed the smiling fields and woods of the Isle of Wight and steamed up Southampton Water. It was a fine bright sunny day, and as we moved into the dock alongside the waiting Hospital Trains, one of the great doorways through which men can return Home from the Great Adventure seemed to open up ahead and bid us welcome.

SIDE SHOWS

I

A Field General Court Martial

WHILE at Neuville St. Vaast I acted one day as Prosecutor at a Field General Court Martial. The accused—Private Alexander M'Graw—while his Battalion was back in billets, had unfortunately drunk too deeply of the vintage of France and eventually fallen foul of the military police. The Court consisted of a Lieut.-Colonel as President, with three other officers as members, and one of these officers was the Corps Court Martial Officer. This officer was in civil life a London barrister, and was now responsible that the proceedings at all Courts Martial within the Corps area were carried through in correct and proper form. Unfortunately he was not well acquainted with the peculiarities of the Scottish dialect as spoken by the accused and witnesses. The N.C.O.s and men giving evidence were rather a dour lot, and the barrister, thinking apparently that the proceedings were not going with sufficient swing, attempted to cheer things up by hurling volleys of questions at the stolid witnesses. This process had only the

SIDE SHOWS

effect of making them less communicative. In addition to launching the attack of interrogations, he was at the same time busily writing down the questions and answers.

Part of his examination of one of the witnesses was something like this:

Court Martial Officer: "When you tried to dissuade him from taking the sixth glass what happened?"

Witness (kilted Scot): "He wudna' tak' a tellin'."

C.M.O. (politely): "I beg your pardon."

Witness: "He said he wud do blinkin' well as he liked."

C.M.O. (struggling to bring matters to a head): "Was the accused drunk or sober?"

Witness (with native caution): "A wudna' say he was drunk, but a wudna' like to say either he was sober."

C.M.O. (deeply imbued by the military principle that there can be no intermediate state between cold sobriety and complete intoxication): "Come, come, he must either have been drunk or sober. Considering your nationality, my man, you seem to know very little about Drink."

Witness (deeply wounded by such a suggestion): "Aye, Sur, and you seem to know very little aboot Saundy M'Graw."

C.M.O. (adopting different tactics): "Will you describe how the accused behaved when he came out of the Estaminet?"

Witness: "A dinna' mind."

C.M.O. (in tones of icy politeness): "Well, as

you are kind enough to say you have no objections to answering my question, please do so."

(Fortunate intervention by the President of the Court, who had been sitting well back in his chair with a quiet smile on his face.)

. . . .

C.M.O. (returning gallantly to the attack): "You say the accused was lying asleep on the stretcher, and that he roused himself and sat up. Now tell the Court what happened next."

Witness: "He jist fell ower again."

C.M.O. (in triumphant tone, believing himself to be hot on the track of new and important evidence): "Ah, he fell over again did he? Now, what did he fall over?"

Witness (now under strong suspicion that his leg is being pulled): "Och away!"

(Collapse of C.M.O. and fortunate resumption of examination by the President.)

II

A Company Concert in Palestine

On a particular evening in May I went up to dine at the Mess of a Company whose Headquarters were on Kurd Hill, and later attended a concert for the men. It was a typical Company concert, and was held in a little wadi with steep sides, into which were burrowed the dugouts of the men. At one point near by a group of dixies with a few bits of wood jealously guarded by a rather grimy-looking gentleman clad in a thin vest and khaki trousers, deeply impregnated with soot and grease, proclaimed itself the Company kitchen. A little further along were stacked piles of leather Lewis gun portmanteaux which carry the ammunition drums. The guns themselves were not there, but a glance into the No. 1's bivouac would assuredly have disclosed them safely tucked away in their covers, for the No. 1 regards his guns with the same mingled pride and affection he might bestow upon his children.

Pitched at a little distance from the other bivouacs—for at all times a proper propriety must be observed—were the temporary dwellings of the Company Sergeant-Major and the Company Quartermaster-Sergeant. Hidden somewhere in the recesses of the latter's shack would no doubt be found the "iron ration" of candles, which is always prima facie evidence that the C.Q.M.S. knows his job. Close beside the kitchen the wadi widens out for a short distance, and here the men were already assembled. They were sitting around on the banks, and those who were lucky enough to have any cigarettes left over from their last issue were inhaling the fragrant "Ruby Queen." The heat of the day was gone with the sun, and the air clear and cool. A lighted candle which flickered uneasily in the gathering darkness, and an empty ration box on which the name "Libby" was branded, showed that the Stage Manager had completed his work.

Then, with the arrival of the officers, the programme began. The C.S.M. was the Master of Ceremonies, and the first performer was Lance-Corporal M'William, who in the piping days of peace had earned the emoluments of a plumber's apprentice in Port Dundas. His selection was "Annie Laurie," and although he ascended the rostrum with a fair outward show of assurance, he was secretly exercised as to the precise point in his vocal range at which to open the engagement. After a preliminary expectoration in the sand, he got his head well back and went "over the top" with a rush. Unfortunately when well under weigh he found that the key had played him false, with the result that at times he appeared to be entirely overcome by emotion, and in spite of valiant efforts to reach his objective, the top notes were left in silence to the imagination. Applause was generous, as was rightly due to one who had made a gallant struggle, but failed in a purpose that was too lofty for his powers.

The next gentleman was Private M'Gurkin, one of the Bad Boys of the Family, whose Conduct Sheet was so frequently required for disciplinary purposes that for convenience sake the Company Commander kept it constantly in his pocket. But he was a cheerful rascal as well as a very gallant man in action, and although he never knew it, he held a larger place in the aforesaid Company Commander's heart than the majority of the others whose conduct sheets contained a less interesting and varied history of crime. His song dealt with such evergreen topics as Mixed Bathing and Mothers-in-law, and from a mere pianissimo of

SIDE SHOWS

suggestiveness worked itself up in a steady crescendo, until about the fourth verse little if anything was left to the imagination. Fortunately Company concerts do not require to be prudish.

Then followed Private Kinstry. He was a signaller, and as such looked down somewhat upon his fellows who were not like himself members of that learned profession. A mouth organ was produced from his trouser pocket, and after wiping his mouth with his tunic sleeve and a preliminary run up the notes in gentle arpeggios, he gave a very creditable rendering of the pantomime songs of three seasons back. It was a most popular turn. Then came the thunderous voice of the Master of Ceremonies, "Order, please, for Mr. Archy." Mr. Archy was an enthusiast, and had managed nearly three years earlier to secure His Majesty's Commission at the ripe age of seventeen. Incidentally he was also the Lewis Gun Officer, and could recite backwards in his sleep all the stoppages to which a gun may fall heir and the detailed methods of correcting each in three seconds. His favourite beverage was Crême-de-Menthe, and in view of his performance he had fortified himself with the contents of two liqueur glasses. His selection was a popular song from a musical comedy, but unfortunately its particular brand of naughtiness was of rather too subtle and elusive a character for the present audience. However, his undoubted popularity with the men drew forth a storm of applause, the loudest bursts of which came from a quarter where I suspected his Lewis gunners were assembled.

The dimensions of the stage were now doubled by the addition of a second ration box, and on the top of this crazy structure Private Square-Pusher, one of the officers' batmen, performed a sand dance to the accompaniment of Private Kinstry's mouth organ. It was really more noteworthy as a balancing feat than as a Terpsichorean achievement, but met with unstinted approval. A lugubrious-looking gentleman, known to his intimates as "old Frisky," came next. The wide bandages on both knees and round his neck hid raw septic sores, for he had been with the Battalion since Gallipoli days, and his blood was thin. Tucking the unexpended portion of his "Ruby Queen" in a place of safety behind his right ear, he tackled the work in hand. His song throughout its ten verses dealt exhaustively with the pleasures of Drink and cognate subjects, the final verse supplying a sort of sub-para on the Delights of Delirium Tremens. The performance contained only the merest hint of a tune, though a touch of realism was introduced by an occasional hiccough, but judging by the applause, it was apparent that the subject matter of the song lay very near the hearts of the audience.

Then came the "Sands of the Desert" (without which no Company concert is complete) delivered, with much fervour and amid heavy intakes of breath, by Corporal M'Phun. One might have thought that a familiarity with this theme trudged out over the miles from Kantara to Gaza might have bred a certain contempt in the audience, but no. The second part of the programme was similar to the first, but always the songs which stirred the audience to their innermost depths and invariably romped home easy winners were those concerning gentlemen or ladies in different stages of intoxication, or any that could hit with heavy sentimental touch such titles as " The Old Home Among the Heather," or " Mother is with the Angels, Daddy." Any others were apt to come in a bad second.

When the musical appetite was nearing repletion the Company Commander called the Master of Ceremonies to his side, and suggested that it was time to get going with " God Save the King." Corporal M'William succeeded in striking a happy key, and a hundred throats sent the strains rolling down the wadi and out into the still desert air.

www.ingramcontent.com/pod-product-compliance
Lightning Source LLC
Chambersburg PA
CBHW052342230426
43664CB00042B/2664